CAUSES OF THE CIVIL WAR

CAUSES OF THE CIVIL WAR

PHILIP LEIGH

SHOTWELL PUBLISHING

Columbia, South Carolina

Produced in the Republic of South Carolina by

Shotwell Publishing, LLC
Post Office Box 2592
Columbia, South Carolina 29202

www.ShotwellPublishing.com

Cover Image: Confederate Soldiers. Courtesy Library of Congress.
Cover Design: Hazel's Dream/Boo Jackson TCB

ISBN: 978-1-947660-41-0

10 9 8 7 6 5 4 3 2 1

CONTENTS

PREFACE

NEARLY ALL HISTORIANS CONTEND that Southerners caused the Civil War by illegally seceding from the United States in order to perpetuate black slavery. The original seven-state Confederacy started the fighting when it bombarded Federally owned Fort Sumter in South Carolina's Charleston Harbor. Northerners virtuously responded by suppressing the Confederate rebellion, which included four additional states after Sumter, thereby ending slavery and intending to establish a more perfect postbellum Union that would provide racial equality for ex-slaves.

Almost all of the above synopsis is wrong or deceptive.

First, secession did not cause the war. Northerners could have evacuated Fort Sumter and let the seven cotton states depart in peace. The reasons why they didn't are seldom investigated. Upon examination, however, it is revealed that Northerners went to war chiefly to avoid the economic consequences of disunion. Among such consequences would have been the effects of a low-tariff Confederacy adjacent to the Federal Union. The overpriced goods of tariff-protected Northern manufacturers would have lost their Southern markets to more efficient European producers. Federal tax revenue, predominantly reliant upon customs duties, would have declined by the amount Southerners paid that was implicit in the price of the imported goods they consumed. Northerners would have lost their legal monopoly on Southern coastal shipping as the seceded states allowed competitors to enter the market. Finally, the

Federal Union would have lost 60% of its exports thereby becoming a perpetual debtor nation to its trading partners.[1]

Second, the alleged illegality of secession is only presumed in retrospect. In 1860 there was no consensus on its legal status. In fact, the Northeastern states threatened secession at least five times during America's first sixty years. The first time was during George Washington's presidency when Treasury Secretary Alexander Hamilton warned that the Northeastern states would secede unless the Federal Government agreed to assume an obligation to pay-off their Revolutionary War debts.

In 1803 New Englanders threatened to secede over the Louisiana Purchase. They worried that the new territories would ultimately become new states thereby reducing New England's influence. A dozen years later they would ask for a constitutional amendment requiring a two-thirds congressional vote before admitting any new state. Regarding the 1803 incident, Senator James Hillhouse of Connecticut warned, "The Eastern states must and will dissolve the union and form a separate government" if they did not get their way. Other notable New Englanders such as John Quincy Adams, Elbridge Gerry, Fisher Ames, Josiah Quincy III, Timothy Pickering, and Joseph Story endorsed his position.[2]

In 1807 New England again threatened secession after America announced a trade embargo, hoping to avoid the War of 1812 by use of economic sanctions. New Englanders objected because their

---

[1] Kenneth Stampp, *And the War Came,* (Baton Rouge: LSU Press, 1950), 218, 223, 225, 227-28, 231-35

[2] Walter Williams, "Historical Ignorance and Confederate Generals," *Town Hall* (July 22, 2020) Available: https://tinyurl.com/y3kfa7st Accessed: [July 22, 2020]; William B. Hesseltine, *A History of the South: 1607-1935* (New York: Prentice Hall, 1936), 174, 176; "Timothy Pickering to George Cabot, January 29, 1804," *The Founders Constitution: Chapter 7, Document 24:* University of Chicago Press: Available: https://tinyurl.com/y8wdewn3 [Accessed: April 26, 2020]; Samuel Elliot Morison and Henry Steel Commager *The Growth of the American Republic: Volume 1,* (New York: Oxford University Press, 1962), 383-84; Thomas Fleming, *A Disease of the Public Mind,* (New York: Da Capo Press, 2013), 82

region was then America's maritime center. After the embargo failed, Congress declared war on Great Britain during President James Madison's first administration but most New Englanders cooperated little in our nation's defense. They traded liberally with the enemy and refused to put their militia into Federal service as ordered by President Madison. When the British finally blockaded New England during the last seven months of the thirty-month war, the region held a convention in Hartford to discuss secession or other steps to protect their interests from Federal powers. In January 1815 the Convention sent emissaries to President Madison to demand five additional constitutional amendments. Upon arriving in Washington, they learned that the war had ended and went home in embarrassment. Soon thereafter their Federalist Party collapsed.[3]

Even as late as 1844 leaders in the Northeastern states threatened to secede over the proposed annexation of Texas. In 1843 twelve congressmen, including former President John Quincy Adams, signed a letter to the people claiming that Texas annexation would not only result in the secession of "free states" but would "fully justify it." A year later former New York Governor and future Secretary of State under Presidents Lincoln and Andrew Johnson, William H. Seward, wrote that the "free-labor states cannot yield" to Texas annexation. They would consider it grounds "for secession, nullification and disunion." The Massachusetts legislature underscored the opinion by declaring the 1845 Texas annexation to be unconstitutional.[4]

In truth, secession was a remedy that geographically isolated political minorities repeatedly considered from 1789 to 1861. As a result, it tended to find favor within those regions that were out-of-power in Washington. It was popular in New England when

---

[3] Samuel Elliot Morison and Henry Steel Commager *The Growth of the American Republic: Volume 1*, 394-96, 427-29

[4] William B. Hesseltine, *A History of the South: 1607-1935*, 303, 306; Thomas Fleming, *A Disease of the Public Mind*, 166-67

Virginians were President, which included all but four years from 1789 to 1825. Conversely, it was popular in the South when Northerners controlled Washington, or merely the House of Representatives where the South never had a majority due to the North's greater population. The House was uniquely important because it was the only place where Congress could originate revenue bills. Once passed, such bills converted into revenue acts thereby becoming tax policy, which was important to everyone.[5]

The third deception in the opening synopsis is that the four states that joined the Confederacy after President Lincoln called for troops to coerce the cotton states back into the Union also seceded to protect slavery. In truth, the four—Virginia, North Carolina, Tennessee and Arkansas—seceded because they had earlier warned Washington that they considered coercion to be unconstitutional and would fight against it. After joining the cotton states, they provided half of the white population from which the eleven-state Confederacy drew nearly all of her soldiers.

A fourth pretext is the assumption that Southern secession was an unacceptable alternative to Civil War because slavery would otherwise have never ended. Historian James Oakes correctly notes in *The Scorpion's Sting*, however, that Northerners and Southerners both realized that slavery would eventually end if it could not grow. But he wrongly assumes that only the Republican Party platform insured that slavery would be isolated in the South. To the contrary, after popular sovereignty demonstrated in 1858 that Kansas could not win admission as a slave state there was no need for a blanket ban on slaves in the territories as Republicans demanded. Popular sovereignty alone would have prevented the admission on any additional slave states because all of the remaining 1860 Federal territories were unsuitable for slave-based agriculture. Moreover, Southerners showed that they would abide

---

[5] Samuel Elliot Morison and Henry Steel Commager *The Growth of the American Republic: Volume 1*, 367

by the decisions of popular sovereignty because it was a specific campaign plank for their 1860 presidential candidate, John C. Breckinridge.

If the Republicans had also adopted popular sovereignty, they could have kept slavery quarantined in the South peacefully. The infant GOP failed to do so because it would have rendered their Party irrelevant and obsolete. That is why Lincoln, as President-elect, refused all compromise proposals.[6]

A fifth dubious presumption is that Southern secession was a bad alternative to preserving the Union militarily. Denying secession required America's bloodiest war. Notwithstanding that the country's 1860 population was only one-fourth that of 1940, more than 700,000 American soldiers died in the Civil War as compared to 400,000 in World War II. President Lincoln ran roughshod over civil liberties, arrested Maryland legislators in order to prevent the state's secession, disbanded Missouri's legislature under the glitter of bayonets, suspended *habeas corpus* in defiance of a contrary ruling by the Chief Justice, shut down opposing newspapers, imprisoned thousands of citizens on political whim without charging them for a crime and manipulated the 1864 soldier vote. The Civil War may not have been worth the cost of the violence done to the Constitution and its irrevocable push toward a progressively more centralized government.[7]

Sixth, historians who point to the *Declarations of Causes* for secession provided by some of the seven cotton states as proof of the primacy of slavery often overlook other differences that are revealed when comparing the U.S.A. and C.S.A. constitutions. Unlike the Federal Constitution, the Confederacy's did not permit

---

[6] James Oakes, *The Scorpion's Sting*, (New York: W. W. Norton, 2014), 26, 36-37, 49-50; J. G. Randall and David Donald, *The Civil War and Reconstruction*, (Boston: D. C. Heath, 1961), 178-79; Democratic Platform, 1860 (Breckinridge faction), https://tinyurl.com/y8mcxcax; Democratic Platform, 1860 (Douglas faction), https://tinyurl.com/r7c3a5m

[7] William Marvel, *Mr. Lincoln Goes to War*, (Boston: Houghton-Mifflin, 2006), xii-xvii

protective tariffs. Southerners were ahead of their time in recognizing the benefits of Worldwide free trade. They also outlawed public works spending, which were instead to be financed by private industry or the states themselves. Since Southerners disliked crony capitalism their constitution prohibited subsidies for private industry, which were allowed under the "general welfare" clause of the Federal Constitution.

The Confederate Constitution only permitted spending for military defense, repayment of national debt, and the operating costs of the Central Government, not pork barrel spending. It also included a number of features that underscored a states' rights philosophy. Constitutional amendments, for example, could only be initiated by a convention of as few as three states, not Congress. The individual states could also impeach Confederate office holders operating entirely within the borders of such states.[8]

Additionally, historians who cite the *Declarations of Causes* to assert the primacy of slavery as a cause of the Civil War, generally fail to note that at least ten Northern free states passed legislative resolutions in December 1860 and January 1861 to explain their objections to Southern secession. Not one stated any wish to abolish Southern slavery. The most consistent complaint was against the resultant breakup of the Union. Thus, Northerners chiefly went to war in order to avoid the economic consequences of disunion, as explained above.[9]

Seventh, the Southern Confederacy was not a rebellion. It had no object to replace the Federal Government in Washington. Everyone knew Southerners would make no attempt to overthrow Lincoln, or

---

[8] *Yale Law School.* "Confederate Constitution." Available: https://tinyurl.com/upv38lx, [Accessed: July 23, 2020]

[9] Philip Leigh, "Northern Response to Southern Secession," *Civil War Chat,* Available: https://tinyurl.com/y7runqtz, [Accessed: July 23, 2020] The ten states were New York, New Jersey, Minnesota, Michigan, Maine, Massachusetts, Ohio, Indiana, Pennsylvania and Wisconsin.

militarily invade the Northern states, if the cotton states had been allowed to depart peacefully.

Eighth, contrary to popular belief, postbellum Northerners were not indulgent toward their defeated foe. They transformed the South into an internal colony to be exploited much like Great Britain did with Ireland. In 1860 the South's per capita income was at the 72nd percentile of the national average. After the Civil War it dropped to the 51st percentile and stayed there for at least thirty-five years. It did not return to its still-below-average 1860 percentile until 1950, ninety years later.[10]

Radical Republicans set up puppet Southern regimes by disfranchising many ex-Confederates and transforming Freedmen into a Republican-loyal voting bloc. They made false promises to the Freedmen and taught them to hate their former masters. When Republican Ulysses Grant was elected President in 1868, he won only a minority of America's white votes and gained the edge in popular vote only because of the ex-slave vote. Postbellum Republicans launched the Gilded Age of crony capitalism by giving away 200 million acres to Northern railroads, which was about twice the property presently within California's borders. Only negligible land grants went to former slaves. By 1877 Republicans had abandoned the blacks because the Party could control Congress and the presidency without them. The "more perfect Union" that Lincoln had hoped to form became one in which black and white Southerners had been dumped into peonage. Even as late as the 1940s both races worked under conditions little different than Russian serfs of the nineteenth century.[11]

---

[10] William J. Cooper and Thomas Terrill *The American South: Volume 2* (Lanham, Md.: Rowman & Littlefield, 2009) 462

[11] David Cohn, *The Life and Times of King Cotton,* (New York: Oxford University Press, 1956), 156; *National Emergency Council: Report on the Economic Conditions of the South,* 46 (July 22, 1938) Available: https://tinyurl.com/ybakbzdt, [Accessed: July 12, 2020]; J. G. Randall and David Donald, *The Civil War and Reconstruction,* 640-41

Finally, the conqueror's version of black civil rights did not include having blacks live among Northerners. In fact, the chief racial goal of Northern whites was to keep blacks out of the North. Since Freedmen comprised a decisive Republican-loyal Southern voting bloc, the infant GOP wanted to keep them there. Simultaneously, Northern workers did not want blacks to cross the Ohio River or the Mason Dixon Line in order to compete for higher paying jobs than were available in the South. Republican Congressman George Boutwell, who later became treasury secretary under President Grant, proposed to reserve the states of South Carolina and Florida exclusively for blacks, even if whites had to be forcibly relocated. Similarly, President Grant attempted to annex the Caribbean island of Santo Domingo, later explaining that he wanted it as a reserve for ex-slaves.[12]

This book reaches different conclusions than those currently dominating our culture for two reasons.

First, and foremost, it is free of academic censorship. History professors and academic presses are intolerant of viewpoints other than their own. Moreover, since nearly all of them agree with one another, they have convinced themselves that their viewpoints are not merely accurate, but uncompromisingly virtuous. During the past thirty-five years they have transplanted their narcissism and intolerance into their students in an apparent egotistical attempt to live forever. Such historians will accept as PhD candidates only those students whose opinions fit into an ever-narrower Overton Window of allowable topics. Consequently, they portray Confederate memorials as subjects of derision and fit objects for mob destruction.

Second, this book examines facts that modern historians ignore or minimize. One example is Breckinridge's popular sovereignty

---

[12] Allen Guelzo, *Redeeming the Great Emancipator,* (Cambridge: Harvard University Press, 2016), 96; Ronald C. White, *American Ulysses,* (New York: Random House, 2016), 513

platform in the 1860 election. Another is the repeated secession threats New Englanders made during the first sixty years of the Republic. A third is consideration of the victor's postbellum conduct as an indicator of antebellum motives. Notwithstanding that pre-war Northerners favored protective tariffs for forty years before the Civil War, for example, academics fail to deduce that the increase in average tariffs from 19% before the war to 45% for fifty years thereafter was an indication of Northern war aims.

Since the popular understanding of Civil War causes has become corrupted, it is best to learn the truth by first identifying the initial cracks in the Federal Union, which date to President Washington's first term.

CHAPTER 1: FOUNDATIONAL CRACKS

THE CAUSES OF THE CIVIL WAR date from the start of the Republic. Writing in 1862 about America's 1787 constitutional convention, Connecticut scholar William Chauncy Fowler explained that the convention nearly fell apart along two fault lines. First, was the North's insistence in having protection for its commerce. Second, was the South's insistence for protection of slavery.

The Northeast dominated commerce, finance, shipping, international trade and the maritime businesses including fishing and shipbuilding. At the 1787 Constitutional Convention "Northerners declared that they had but one motive to form a Constitution, and that was *commerce*," according to Fowler. To avoid becoming even more tributary to Northeastern business, Southerners wanted to require a two-thirds congressional majority for passage of any new "navigation" (i.e. shipping, trade and tariff) laws. Failing to get such a provision, by the 1820s they found themselves bound hand-and-foot to any commerce law desired by an unsympathetic President and simple congressional majority. The Northern states always held a majority in the House of Representatives where the Constitution requires that revenue bills originate.

Conversely, the six southernmost of the thirteen states had 94% of America's slaves. Although the overall population was split fifty-fifty between North and South, House of Representatives

1

membership tilted 57%-to-43% in favor of the North because Northerners secured a constitutional provision that excluded two-fifths of any state's slave population for purposes numbering her congressmen and calculating her electoral votes. In exchange, Southerners were able include a Fugitive Slave clause in the Constitution requiring the return of runaway slaves. More importantly, Fowler observes, "The Constitution was intended to secure to the Southern States peaceable possession of their slaves; and had it not been supposed that it did so, it would never have been adopted by them."[13]

There were other intersectional differences besides slavery and commerce. One Virginia constitutional convention delegate, George Mason, refused to sign the document because he feared the resultant Central Government would forever grow, eventually marginalizing the states. He felt that the Constitution would be transformed into an instrument used by the commercial North to exploit the agricultural South. Considering man's natural lust for control, he argued, "I fear the thirst for power will prevail to oppress the people." Although a planter, Mason opposed slavery and had freed his own slaves. Fellow Virginian and slavery opponent Patrick Henry worried that the Northern majority might impose unfair taxation. Even though the ratification tide was against him, Mason argued successfully for safeguards that would ultimately become the Bill of Rights amendments ratified after the Constitution was adopted in 1789.[14]

Despite similar misgivings in other states, Americans accepted the Constitution mostly because they knew that George Washington favored it and he would likely become the first President. Soon after

---

[13] William Fowler, *The Sectional Controversy* (New York: Charles Scribner, 1864), 14-15, 22-23, 27-28

[14] Francis Simkins and Charles Roland, *A History of the South,* (New York: Alfred A. Knopf, 1972), 87-88; United States Census, 1790, Available: https://tinyurl.com/jh54sbn [Accessed: April 29, 2020]

the 57-year-old Washington took office in April 1789 he assembled a group of four younger men to help him form the Federal Government. The two most influential were New York's 32-year-old Alexander Hamilton and Virginia's 46-year-old Thomas Jefferson. Hamilton was the Treasury Secretary and Jefferson the Secretary of State. During 1790-91 Hamilton wrote a series of reports proposing four initiatives.

First, was to fund the national debt issued under the 1777 Articles of Confederation with new bond issues of the Federal Government. The bill would also assume the Revolutionary War debts of the individual states. Second, was to pass an excise tax to support the government. A fiscally responsible General Government had never been achieved under America's earlier Confederation Articles. Third, was to form a national bank. Fourth, was to adopt import tariffs in order to protect domestic industries from overseas competition and to pay down the soon-to-be acquired Federal debts.

Hamilton sought to bind America's commercial interests to the Federal Government. He had little respect for the common man, whom he considered tributary to the commercial and privileged sectors. "All communities," he argued, "were composed of the few and the many. The first are the rich and well-born; the other the mass of the people . . . turbulent and changing, they seldom judge or determine the right. Give, therefore, to the first class a distinct, permanent share of the government." Accordingly, he wanted to restrict voting rights.[15]

Except for tariffs, which Congress had already passed, Hamilton got everything he wanted. Northern speculators in Continental debts, centered in Hamilton's New York, reaped big gains when the Federal Government refunded the debts at face value with new bonds. Speculators had purchased some of the refunded bonds for

---

[15] William B. Hesseltine, *A History of the South: 1607-1935*, 171-73

as little at 12% of face value. A whisky excise tax also helped pay the Federal debt, but it was unpopular west of the Alleghenies where coin was scarce and jars of distilled spirts sometimes functioned as money. Business centers like New York were relieved that the bond refunding and excise taxes gave the new country stable credit, which the region would need if it were to become a center of international trade. New England benefitted from the tariffs and tonnage fees on foreign shipping.

Alexander Hamilton

Although Hamilton's program helped the North, it hurt the South. Southerners protested at redeeming the Continental and state debts at face value. Virginia and North Carolina particularly complained because they had already donated large land tracts to the Federal Government. The grants included much of the present-day Midwest together with Tennessee and Kentucky. Congressional debates over the Debt Assumption Bill were so heated that some representatives of Northeastern states told Hamilton their states would secede if it did not pass. Thus, the first secession threat came from the North, not the South. Eventually, Hamilton beguiled Jefferson by promising to help relocate the national capital to the Potomac River instead of leaving it in Pennsylvania. In exchange, Jefferson agreed to support the bill. Soon afterward, however, Jefferson regretted the deal when he learned of the extraordinary profits gained by the Northeastern "stock jobbing herd."[16]

Shortly after Washington's 1789 inauguration and well before Hamilton released his protective tariff manifesto, Virginia Congressman and House Speaker James Madison got a tariff bill enacted. Known alternately as the Tonnage Act or Tariff Act, Madison's law put a 50-cent per ton duty on the cargo capacity of foreign ships entering U.S. ports whereas American-owned vessels were charged only 6-cents. The act also specified import duties ranging from 5% to 15% on an itemized list of imports. Although low by later standards, Madison's tariff protected domestic manufacturers and also provided revenue to operate the Federal Government and paydown the assumed Continental and state debts.

Despite similarities, tonnage fees and tariffs are different, although both benefitted the Northeast where the maritime and trading interests were centered. Tariffs are customs duties on a list of specific items, whereas tonnage fees apply to the entire ship. The latter are calculated by multiplying a per-ton rate by the weight of water displaced by the ship. They also tended to yield a monopoly on intercoastal trade to American hulls because a foreign ship was required to pay tonnage fees at each American port it entered. A British ship that delivered cargo to New York where it bought wheat that it delivered to Charleston, for example, would need to pay two tonnage fees.

In the vocabulary of tariff taxation, the 1789 Tariffs were a mix of revenue and *protective* duties. *Revenue* tariffs were designed to raise money, not protect any domestic industry from overseas competition by deterring imports. Duties on coffee are a classic example because the beans are not produced in any state but consumed in all of them. In contrast, a protective tariff is

---

[16] *Ibid.*, 174, 176; William Fowler, *The Sectional Controversy*, 36-37

deliberately written to insulate targeted domestic producers from foreign competition. Any tax revenue it may provide is secondary. In fact, the optimal protective tariff raises no money because it blocks all imports of the specified item leaving the American producer with a domestic monopoly. It was the monopolistic aspects of protective tariffs that Southerners found most objectionable, well into the twentieth century.

Hamilton urged liberal use of protective tariffs so that the United States could grow into a manufacturing empire with little dependence on agriculture. But protective tariffs injured America's export regions, such as the South. Foreign buyers of cotton and tobacco needed to sell manufactured goods into American markets in order to earn the dollars required to buy American agricultural exports. Protective tariffs impede such exchange-generating imports. The detrimental effect of high tariffs on agricultural exports became one of the South's major objections to protective tariffs for the North's manufactured goods. When European imports were artificially restricted by tariffs, Europe had fewer dollars to pay for American exports. That had the effect of reducing the quantity of export goods foreigners could buy and/or the price they could pay. The impact was most obvious on America's commodity exports such as cotton. Even though tariffs represented 90% of Federal revenues until the Civil War, most modern historians fail to appreciate their importance in causing the Civil War, as shall be explained.

Madison conceded that the 1789 tariffed articles "were pretty generally taxed for the benefit of the manufacturing part of the northern community." He also admitted that the South— then the main wealth-producing part of the nation—would inevitably "shoulder a disproportionate share of the financial burden involved in transforming the United States into a commercial, manufacturing, and maritime power." Nonetheless, he was willing to make such sacrifices for the benefit of the entire Union. While the tonnage fees decidedly favored American shipping, Northerners still wanted higher tariffs. Thus, tariff fights became annual rituals and twenty-five tariff laws were passed between 1792 and 1816.[17]

* * *

Although Benjamin Franklin had earlier owned slaves and even paid to have a runaway returned, after the Federal Government became operational, he asked Congress to restrict slavery. Congress responded with a resolution stating that it had no power to interfere with slavery in any state but also affirmed its authority over interstate slave trade. Ultimately, Franklin's request resulted in the 1793 Fugitive Slave Act.

It was enacted after Maryland slave catchers captured a free Pennsylvania black and Maryland declined to honor Pennsylvania's request for rendition of the alleged kidnappers. Consequently, Pennsylvania lobbied for a Federal law to protect her free black residents. The resultant 1793 Act became the means of implementing the Constitution's Fugitive Slave clause. It provided that a white man claiming a black as a slave should satisfactorily prove his claim before a state or federal magistrate who was empowered to issue a warrant for the fugitive's arrest. Although later weakened by an 1842 Supreme Court ruling, the 1793 Act would remain effective until a new Fugitive slave law was enacted in 1850. The '93 Act's provisions were effectively executed until the 1830s when New England's commercial interests adopted abolitionism as a trick tool for attacking Southerners who opposed protective tariffs. By criticizing slavery, New Englanders could hit their tariff opponents in a morally vulnerable spot.[18]

---

[17] John C. Miller, *The Federalist Era,* (New York: Harper & Row, 1963) 17-18; F. W. Taussig, *A Tariff History of the United States,* (New York: G. P. Putnam, 1905), 14-16; William Hill, "Prospective Purpose of the Tariff Act of 1789," *Journal of Political Economy,* V.2, N. 1 (December 1893): 58; William Benson, *A Political History of the Tariff,* (Bloomington, In.: Xlibris, 2010), 15

[18] William B. Hesseltine, *A History of the South: 1607-1935,* 173; William Fowler, *The Sectional Controversy,* 29

For the rest of Washington's two presidential terms sectional differences focused upon the relative powers of the Federal and state governments. New York's Hamilton took the lead for the former and Virginia's Jefferson for the latter. Their differences became evident when Washington asked his cabinet for opinions on a national bank bill. Along with Madison who authored much of the Constitution, Jefferson maintained that the foundational document did not give Congress a specific power to charter a bank. In contrast, Hamilton argued that a national bank was legitimate because the Constitution granted Congress the right to make all laws "necessary and proper" for executing its power to levy taxes and emit bills of credit. After Washington sided with Hamilton the First Bank of the United States was chartered for a twenty-year term in February 1791. Like fellow Virginian John Marshall who would become Chief Supreme Court Justice in 1801, Washington tilted toward a liberal interpretation of Federal authority along with Hamilton whereas Jefferson was a strict constructionist.[19]

By 1796 both Jefferson and Hamilton were out of the cabinet. While Hamilton figuratively remained the power behind the throne Jefferson proceeded to organize an opposition party. Although both men wanted to become the country's second President, the honor went Massachusetts' John Adams who had been Washington's Vice President. After the South started regularly opposing Hamilton's centralization philosophy, it united behind Jefferson who became Adams's Vice President. Jefferson's stature as a Hamilton opponent grew during the Adams Administration because Hamilton and Adams often quarreled. Resentment between the two Northerners lingered after Adams's election because Hamilton had tried to persuade some electors to switch their votes to Adams's running mate, Thomas Pinckney, which would have made Pinckney the second President. Ultimately events during the Adams years would

---

[19] William B. Hesseltine, *A History of the South: 1607-1935*, 178-79; Francis Simkins and Charles Roland, *A History of the South*, 89

8

cause Jefferson to become the chief proponent of the Compact Theory of the Federal Union, a basis for arguing the legality of nullification and secession.

After Adams became President, America came into contact with the unstable regimes that followed the French Revolution. Adams and his Federalist Party were sickened by the anarchy and violence that characterized France after 1792. They worried that French revolutionaries might emigrate to America and try to overthrow our government. Consequently, in 1798 Adams pushed the Alien and Sedition Acts through Congress in order to squelch such political movements if they

Thomas Jefferson as Vice President

tried to take root in America. The Sedition Act, for example, made it a crime to "maliciously" criticize the President or Congress.

A number of persons were tried and convicted under the acts, often for trivial offenses. Nevertheless, Federal judges enforced the laws zealously. To Jefferson, such conduct confirmed his fear that the Central Government would become tyrannical. Adams's conduct suggested that New Englanders wanted America to be ruled as a semi-monarchy. Conversely, Jefferson and his allies perceived that the courts were becoming agencies of oppression and destroying the liberties of the people.

As a result, Madison and Jefferson prepared a series of resolutions for the Virginia and Kentucky legislatures that formalized the Compact Theory. It held that the Constitution was a collective compact among individual sovereign states, which implied that the states could nullify illegal congressional acts by right of the constitutional principle of checks and balances. Jefferson argued that as a compact, the Constitution delegated only assigned powers to the Federal Government and "when-so-ever the General Government assumes undelegated powers its acts are unauthoritative, void and of no force." Although the resolutions were officially the positions of only two states, they were based upon the 1791 Tenth Amendment's allocation of residual powers to the states. Therefore, the Virginia and Kentucky resolutions became the bedrock of the states' rights doctrine, a stand that made Jefferson popular enough in the South to narrowly win him the 1800 presidential election. Jefferson's victory left Northeasterners feeling that the Central Government had been taken out of the hands of the Hamiltonian elite and turned over to rabble.[20]

Despite Jefferson's election, future Supreme Court rulings would increasingly try to enlarge the power of the Federal Government. As shall be explained in the next chapter, one case involved James Madison when he was Jefferson's Secretary of State and he denied that "the Federal judiciary" was the ultimate judge of limits for the Central Government. Instead, it was the people of the states themselves. In his earlier Virginia Resolutions Madison wrote, "However true . . . it may be that the [Federal] judicial department is . . . to decide the last resort, this resort must necessarily be deemed the last [only] in relation to the authorities of the other departments of the [Federal] government; not in relation to the rights of the parties [people of the states] . . . to the constitutional compact, from which [all Federal departments] . . . hold their delegated trusts." That the Supreme Court might rule to the contrary was irrelevant.[21]

---

[20] William B. Hesseltine, *A History of the South: 1607-1935*, 180-86; William Fowler, *The Sectional Controversy*, 44, 53

[21] James Madison, *The Writings of James Madison: 1790-1802*, (Boston: G. P. Putnam, 1906), 352

Within America's first dozen years the limits on states' rights had become—and would remain—a defining issue. As Shelby Foote put it, today we unconsciously use a singular verb when constructing a sentence about our country as in, "The United States is . . ." whereas during her first seventy years our ancestors spoke of her as "The United States are. . ." It took the America's bloodiest war to change "are" to "is."

CHAPTER 2: SHAPING STATES' RIGHTS

WHILE THOMAS JEFFERSON was President from 1801 to 1809 it became increasingly clear that states' rights principles might become the shield for most any geographic minority, including the North. Historians Henry Steele Commager and Samuel Morison wrote, "Almost every man in public life between 1798 and 1860 spurned it when his section was in the ascendency and embraced it when his constituents deemed themselves oppressed. Almost every state in turn declared its own absolute sovereignty, only to denounce as treasonable similar declarations by other states." In the end, it was a game of musical chairs. Whenever a regional minority felt that they could never regain the majority they worried that their constitutional rights might be trampled by a tyrannical simple majority in the Central Government. Consequently, they felt they might ultimately need to interpose states' rights even so far as nullification and secession. By 1861 the South was caught without a chair in the game when the music stopped. Under different circumstances it could have been the North.[22]

Jefferson's presidency demonstrated that even political conservatives were prone to expand executive powers when they held them. His critics cite the Louisiana Purchase as an example of constitutional overreach. But if Jefferson stretched, it was with a rubber band compared to the bungee cord Adams had used with his Sedition Act.

---

[22] Morison and Commager *The Growth of the American Republic: Volume 1*, 367

When Washington took office, the Mississippi River was America's western border. After 1789, pioneers moved across the Appalachians to settle in the valleys of the Ohio, Cumberland and Tennessee rivers where they became dependent upon trade through New Orleans. As Spain and France argued over control of Louisiana, trade policies in New Orleans shifted unpredictably. Sometimes Americans got reasonable access and sometimes were charged excessive fees. As a result, Jefferson concluded that America must buy New Orleans. After lengthy negotiations, his envoys were instead given a chance to buy the entire Louisiana Territory for $15 million. By including all lands draining into the Mississippi from the west, Louisiana stretched to the Rocky Mountains and doubled the size of the country. Less than one percent of the area was settled.

Although Jefferson realized that the Constitution did not explicitly give him power to purchase new territories, he felt justified accepting France's ephemeral offer, which could be constitutionally validated as a treaty with a two-thirds vote in the Senate. On October 20, 1803 Jefferson won a decisive 24-to-7 Senate vote. Two months later America took possession of the territory.

The seven Senators who voted against ratification were from Delaware and New England. Although officially objecting that Jefferson lacked constitutional authority to buy the land, their true complaint was that the vast territory would inevitably result in the addition of more states thereby reducing the influence of their own states in the Federal Government. Some argued for secession. Massachusetts Senator Timothy Pickering wrote Boston Brahmin George Cabot in January 1803, "The principles of our Revolution point to the remedy—a separation." Pickering, even argued that

Jefferson would constitutionally need approval of every state in the Union in order to legally purchase Louisiana.[23]

According to historians Morison and Commager, "Before 1803 was out . . . Massachusetts . . . and Connecticut began to plan a Northern Confederacy, in Pickering's words, 'exempt from the corrupting influence and oppression of the aristocratic democrats of the South': a confederacy with New England as a nucleus. . . Knowledge of this conspiracy was confined to the inner circle of New England federalism and the British minister at Washington who gave it his blessing." The conspirators next approached New York's Aaron Burr, who Jefferson had dropped as a running mate for his 1804 re-election. "We know very little for certain what went on; it seems highly probable that, in return for Federalist aid to elect him governor, Burr agreed, if successful, to swing New York into the Northern Confederacy and become its President." Evidently, Alexander Hamilton discovered the plan and urged followers to vote against Burr, which prevented Burr from becoming New York's governor thereby collapsing the scheme. The two men famously dueled on July 11, 1804. Although Hamilton reportedly fired first harmlessly into the air, Burr's aim was true. Hamilton died the following day.[24]

Eight years later in 1811, when a bill was introduced to admit Louisiana as a state, Massachusetts Congressman Josiah Quincy addressed the House: "If this bill passes, it is my deliberate opinion . . . that it is virtually a dissolution of the Union; . . . it will be the right of all, so it will be the duty of some, to prepare for separation, amicably if they can, violently if they must." The Massachusetts legislature echoed Quincy with a resolution stating, ". . . it is the

---

[23] "Timothy Pickering to George Cabot, January 29, 1804," *The Founders Constitution: Chapter 7, Document 24*: University of Chicago Press: Available: https://tinyurl.com/y8wdewn3 [Accessed: April 26, 2020]; Thomas Fleming, *A Disease in the Public Mind*, 92

[24] Morison and Commager *The Growth of the American Republic: Volume 1*, 383-84

interest and duty of the people of Massachusetts to oppose the admission of such states [Louisiana] . . . as a measure tending to dissolve the Confederacy [Federal Union.][25]

After the execution of Louis XVI in 1793, radical France and conservative Britain competed for influence in Europe. The result was the 1799-1815 Napoleonic Wars which had a significant impact on America's economy—initially favorable but later detrimental. Our 1793 Proclamation of Neutrality gave American ships unfettered access to all countries including Britain and France. Freight earnings boomed. In 1792, American shippers earned $7.2 million. By 1796 revenues had tripled to $21.6 million and eventually peaked at $42.1 million in 1807. No region benefitted more than the Northeast.

Aaron Burr

Eventually, however, the two European belligerents interfered with U.S. shipping. Since Napoleon conquered much of continental Europe, the British concluded that they must defeat him by cutting off his supplies. Starting in 1807 any ships bound for France were obliged to stop first in Britain to register and pay a tariff. Additionally, since wartime deserters rendered the British fleet under-maned, whenever an American merchantman crossed paths with a shorthanded British

---

[25] William Fowler, *The Sectional Controversy*, 60

warship, the British ship was apt to impress suspected deserters. In 1807 an unusual impressment happened between a British warship and an American one in Chesapeake Bay. When the USS *Chesapeake* refused to let sailors from HMS *Leopard* board the *Chesapeake* to search for British deserters the *Leopard* fired three broadsides into the *Chesapeake*. Consequently, four American sailors were killed and another four seized as suspected British deserters. The incident was a stinging insult to American honor.

Instead of going to war, President Jefferson first tried economic pressure. Specifically, he persuaded Congress to adopt a trade embargo with all foreign countries in December 1807, escalating the 1806 Non-Importation Act that forbade British imports into the U.S.A. The fourteen-month embargo had little effect on Great Britain, although it enraged Northeastern maritime and commercial interests. In fact, the British merchant marine welcomed the embargo because it removed American vessels as competitors in Global shipping markets. When the ban caused a shortage of provisions in the French West Indies, Napoleon confiscated all American ships that entered any French port.

As a result, New Englanders condemned the Embargo Act as unconstitutional and attacked Jefferson by throwing the 1798 Virginia and Kentucky resolutions back in his face. The Connecticut legislature proclaimed it their duty "to interpose their protecting shield between the right . . . of the people, and the assumed power of the General Government." Boston leaders wrote the state legislature in January 1809: "Our hope and consolation rest with the Legislature . . . to whom it is competent to devise means of relief against the unconstitutional measures of the General Government; that your power is adequate to this object, is evident from the organization of the Confederacy." In September 1808 the *Boston Sentinel* wrote, "If petitions do not produce a . . . removal of the embargo . . . the government of Massachusetts has also a duty to perform. The state is still sovereign and independent." In objecting to the embargo, a Connecticut senator addressed the chamber, "the people [of my state] are not bound to submit and . . . in my opinion, they will not submit." Before James Madison assumed the presidency in March 1809, New Englanders were discussing a convention to regionally nullify the embargo. The threat worked. Three days before leaving office Jefferson rushed a bill through Congress rescinding the embargo.[26]

For the first 23 of the 30-month war that started in June 1812, New England prospered because the British did not blockade her ports until May 1814. As a result, the region traded freely with Canada's Maritime provinces, or overland from Vermont to Quebec despite being at war with them. Moreover, much of imports that arrived in New England were taken to the Middle Atlantic and Southern states in ox carts or sleds in a profit making venture. Since the British blockade also caused a shortage of imported manufactured goods in the rest of the country, New England started becoming a domestic manufacturing center. In 1810 the region had 87,000 cotton spindles, but five years later 130,000 were operating.

Notwithstanding the region's prosperity, the traditional maritime interests complained. Most were members of the Federalist Party that controlled all New England states by 1813. Up to that time their opposition to James Madison's Republican Party had been individual rather than collective. In 1813, however, they began to resist Madison as a cooperative group of regional states. Military enlistments were discouraged, and militias refused to be nationalized to fight the War of 1812.

After years of speculative discussion concerning a regional convention to make a concerted protest, the Hartford Convention materialized near the end of 1814. Its purpose was to revise America's Constitution by providing amendments to increase the region's political power in the General Government. There were two wings of delegates: radical and conservative. The radicals, such as

---

[26] Morison and Commager *The Growth of the American Republic: Volume 1*, 394-96; William Fowler, *The Sectional Controversy*, 59, 63

Timothy Pickering, Josiah Quincy and John Lowell, wanted to draft a new Constitution and present it only to the original thirteen states plus Vermont thereby leaving the newer western states out of the Federal Union. The conservatives wanted to call a convention of all United States to adopt new amendments intended to weaken the power of the South and increase that of the North.

Eventually the Convention settled upon recommendations for five new amendments to the U.S. Constitution. The first would prohibit the Federal Government from adopting a trade embargo lasting more than sixty days. The second would require a two-thirds congressional vote to admit any new state, declare an offensive war, or intercede with foreign commerce. A third would entirely disqualify a state's slave residents for purposes of calculating her number of congressmen and electoral votes. A fourth would limit future presidents to a single term and fifth would require that each new President be from a different state than his predecessor.

The Convention selected three members to carry its message to Washington in January 1815. Before they departed, however, the Convention also resolved to hold a second meeting if the "present evils" continue "without prospect of relief." The resolution also stated that the second meeting's purpose would be to discuss the "dissolution of the Union" and the formation of "a new form of Confederacy." In citing its grievances, the Convention declared that, "acts of Congress in violation of the Constitution are absolutely void."

Justice John Marshall

When the three commissioners arrived in Washington news of the Treaty of Ghent ending the War of 1812, and Andrew Jackson's decisive victory in New Orleans, had preceded them. Since peace would end the British blockade, New England's shipbuilding and maritime interests would return to normal thereby mollifying complaints pertinent to two of the proposed amendments. Given a satisfactory end to the war, insistence upon the other three would make the commissioners and their region appear unpatriotic and selfish. Consequently, they went home having accomplished nothing but embarrassing the Federalist Party, which went into decline and soon vanished.[27]

The secrecy of the Hartford Convention's proceedings—there was purposely no transcript—enabled delegates to consider radical interposition and states' rights principles as a means of blocking unconstitutional acts by the General Government. The delegates were distinguished men and they consulted experts. Among such consultants was New York's Gouverneur Morris. Beyond merely participating in America's 1787 Constitutional Convention, Morris revised its final language. At Hartford he opined that the Constitution is a compact among states and not a compact among individuals scattered across America. The latter was the chief argument used by nullification and secession opponents. While the Hartford Convention was forming, he wrote a Connecticut respondent, "You will unite with Massachusetts, and New York must connect herself with New England. The question of boundary to be solved [for our new confederation], therefore, is the Delaware, Susquehanna, or Potomac [rivers.]"[28]

Since the Federalist Party traditionally favored a strong Central Government, Virginia Congressman John Randolph wrote to

[27] William Fowler, *The Sectional Controversy*, 66; Morison and Commager *The Growth of the American Republic: Volume 1*, 427-29
[28] William Fowler, *The Sectional Controversy*, 68

apprise former Federalist Massachusetts Senator James Lloyd that: "the doctrines of states' rights as enunciated by Northern statesmen and Southern statesmen, are substantially the same."

> 1.The Constitution is a compact among the states, made by the people of the individual states. Thus, the people of a state may remove it from the Union.
>
> 2. It was formed for the states and for individuals only as citizens of a state.
>
> 3. All powers not directly given to the federal government are reserved for the states.
>
> 4. Each state is obliged to judge for itself any violation of the compact.
>
> 5. If a dispute should arise between a state and its co-states concerning the powers that are delegated versus those reserved, a constitutional amendment must settle the point.
>
> 6. If the compact be broken on one side, it is broken on all sides. Therefore, if the Federal Government passes an unconstitutional law, the compact is broken for all states, thus justifying nullification.[29]

Three years earlier, New York Lieutenant Governor Dewitt Clinton critized New England's growing secession sentiment. In an 1811 speech before the New York Senate he said, "The legislatures of the different [New England] states are invited to array themselves against the general government. The very men who a few years since were the strenuous advocates for melting down the State governments, for a strong national executive, that would maintain the union of States; . . . these men now are the war partisans of State supremacy. . . The resolutions of Boston are more seditious than any that were passed" during Pennsylvania's 1791-

---

[29] *Ibid.*, 72

94 Whisky Rebellion. "[They] are certainly intended to infuse a spirit of treason . . ."[30]

In order to have avoided the 1860-61 Southern secession, William Fowler wrote in 1862, "The reserved rights of the States need to be constantly kept before the minds of those who are called to act in the General Government, lest they should lose their influences and the granted powers [of the Federal Government] become . . . too much enlarged. There is a strong centralizing tendency, arising from the love of power, which is inherent in human nature, from a desire to carry out certain measures deemed useful, but which the Constitution does not authorize; and especially from the great patronage of the Government, which it can use to induce men to support its usurpation."[31]

From 1789 to 1815 while Northerners and Southerners alternately raised the states' rights shield to interpose between an unconstitutional Federal action and the people of a given state, the Supreme Court made a number of decisions favoring Federalism. Its growing tendency to strengthen the powers of the Central Government warrants analysis.

According to the Constitution, the power of the Federal Courts "shall extend to all cases . . . arising under this Constitution and the Laws of the United States; . . . to Controversies between two or more States; between a State and Citizens of another State;" Despite such language the states persistently argued that they need not accept the Supreme Court as the final arbiter. They questioned its jurisdiction over sovereign states. Since the Court was a branch of the Federal Government many Americans believed that its rulings had an organic bias toward that government.[32]

---

[30] Jacob Barker, *The Life of Jacob Barker,* (Washington City: Privately Published, 1855), 29-30

[31] William Fowler, *The Sectional Controversy,* 74

[32] Constitution of the United States, Available: https://tinyurl.com/qevw4br [Accessed:

Only four years after George Washington took office in 1789 the 1793 *Chisholm v. Georgia* Supreme Court ruling threatened state sovereignty. In 1792, South Carolina resident Alexander Chisholm sued the State of Georgia over payments for goods supplied to Georgia during the Revolutionary War. The defendant, Georgia, refused to appear. She claimed that as a sovereign state, she could not be sued without consenting to the suit. Due to the courts tendency to increase its own power, it ruled against Georgia. It was only a temporary victory for those favoring centralization. The states quickly and overwhelmingly responded by adopting the Eleventh Amendment in 1795 which stated, "The judicial power of the United States shall not . . . extend to any suit . . . against one of the [states] by citizens of another state."[33]

The Chisholm decision awakened the largely dormant concerns of political conservatives. During the 1787 Constitutional Convention debates, Antifederalists (conservatives) were reluctant to authorize inferior Federal courts. They preferred that state courts handle minor cases. They were especially concerned that the lifetime appointment of Federal judges would tend to make them aristocratic, if they were not already aristocrats when chosen. Beginning in 1791 the Antifederalists came under the leadership of Jefferson and Madison and changed their name to the Democrat-Republicans. (When Andrew Jackson became President in 1828 the Party became known simply as Democrat and was opposed by Whigs. Thereafter, Democrats were generally the Party of commoners and Whigs that of aristocrats.) While Federalists (liberals) supported a Federal court's right of judicial review, the Democrat-Republicans believed that a law's unconstitutionality could only be determined by the states because they were not self-serving instruments of the Central Government.

April 29, 2020]

[33] Oyez.org, Available: https://tinyurl.com/y5e38cx6 [Accessed: April 29, 2020]

When Jefferson became President in 1801, he was annoyed with the Judiciary Act passed late in President Adams's term. Even though his Party might control Congress and the presidency during his administration, the Act insured that the Federalists would control the judiciary because Adams appointed many of the judges for life tenure. When Jefferson directed that Secretary of State Madison not deliver a commission to one of Adams's appointees named William Marbury, the latter sued. In the 1803 *Marbury v. Madison* case Chief Justice Marshall struck down the part of the law that required Madison to issue the commission. It was not, however, a victory for Jefferson and Madison because Marshall's ruling also asserted the Court's authority to rule on the constitutionality of a Federal law. It established the principle of Judicial Review that has ever since enabled the Supreme Court to rule on the constitutionality of any law. The ruling defied the Virginia and Kentucky Resolutions that Madison and Jefferson wrote only five years earlier, reserving the power for deciding a law's constitutionality to the states.

Jefferson felt compelled to reply by explaining that Marshall's ruling contradicted the checks-and-balances constitutional principle. He wrote, "The Constitution on this hypothesis [ruling] is a mere thing of wax in the hands of the judiciary, which they may twist and shape into any form they please." Nonetheless, Marshall continued to issue decisions further narrowing states' rights. His rulings in *Fletcher v. Peck, Cohen v. Virginia* and *McCulloch v. Maryland* limited the powers of state legislatures. Although Jefferson grumbled, he did nothing concrete to combat the Court. His actions never went beyond protest. Marshall would continue to be Chief Justice until 1831. After 1815 most of the Court's rulings favoring Federalism would redound to the benefit of the North.[34]

---

[34] William B. Hesseltine, *A History of the South: 1607-1935*, 197-98

CHAPTER 3: THE SUN SHINES NORTH

NEW ENGLAND'S ECONOMY strengthened during the War of 1812. Not only did she lead foreign trade while other American ports were blockaded, she also became America's manufacturing center. Since Americans could not import manufactured goods customarily obtained from Europe, New England and other Northeastern states started manufacturing domestic substitutes. A prime example was cotton textiles, which was a booming industry for most of the nineteenth century. Once cotton agriculture became economical after the cotton gin invention provided a fifty-to-one improvement for removing seeds, the American South became the dominant Worldwide supplier of feedstock. Cotton production had increased from 85 million pounds in 1810 to 100 million in 1815 and 255 million in 1825. As per-pound prices dropped with production increases, cotton became a favored choice for clothing compared to alternatives such as wool, buckskin, linen, and silk. The number of spindles operating in the domestic cotton textile manufacturing industry increased from 87,000 in 1810 to 130,000 in 1815 and 800,000 in 1825.

When the British withdrew the blockade after the war ended in 1815, cheaper European manufactured goods started returning to the American market. Notwithstanding that America's wartime tariffs were double those of the 1804 Tariff, the new European imports threatened domestic producers. Among the hardest-hit sectors were iron, cotton goods, and woolen goods. Consequently, industrial production declined by 7% in 1816 as vulnerable firms shut down.

Southerners who had traditionally opposed protective tariffs warmed to increases for two reasons. First was the emergence of an

Era of Good Feelings reflecting a unified sense of national purpose that accompanied the end of the War of 1812, alternately referred to as America's Second War of Independence. President Madison's successor, James Monroe, deliberately minimized partisanship with appointments intended to promote geographic unity. Even Thomas Jefferson, who considered himself an agriculturalist, showed that he appreciated the contributions of Northern manufacturers to the war effort when he wrote, "We must now place the manufacturer by the side of the agriculturalist."[35]

A second reason Southerners became more willing to accept protective tariffs was that a younger breed of Southern politicians hoped that their region might also diversify its economy with manufacturing industries. The most significant among such men was House Speaker Henry Clay of Kentucky, who would influence future President Abraham Lincoln's economic policies. Clay wanted America to become more self-reliant. His method to reach that goal was to deter imports with new protective tariffs. Even Congressman John C. Calhoun hoped that deterrence tariffs would provide manufacturing opportunities in his state of South Carolina.[36]

Influenced by the spirit of national unity, in 1815 President Madison urged that the high wartime tariffs remain in force until Congress could craft a protective tariff for the post-war years. Support was strongest in the Middle Atlantic but even Southerners acquiesced so that the country would have its own industrial base

---

[35] Niles' Weekly Register, (Baltimore, Niles Register, 1816), Available: https://tinyurl.com/yajwq2of [Accessed: May 3, 2020]; Douglas Irwin, *Clashing Over Commerce: A History of U. S. Trade Policy* (Chicago: University of Chicago Press, 2017), 125; Scott Corbett, Volker Janssen, John M. Lund, Todd Pfannestiel, Paul Vickery, and Sylvie Waskiewicz, "The Economics of Cotton," *OER Services: U. S. History,* Available: https://tinyurl.com/y35fjnwk [Accessed: May 10, 2020]; F. W. Taussig, *A Tariff History of the United States,* 28; U. S. Department of Commerce. "Historical Statistics of the United Sates: Colonial Times to 1957." Washington: U. S. Government Printing Office, 1960. Available: https://tinyurl.com/yc8mvmld [Accessed: July 26, 2020]; James L. Watkins, *Production and the Price of Cotton for 100 Years,* (Washington: U.S. Govt. Printing Office, 1895), 7-9

[36] H. W. Brands, *Heirs of the Founders,* (New York: Doubleday, 2018), 68-72; William B. Hesseltine, *A History of the South: 1607-1935,* 210, 230; Francis Simkins and Charles Roland, *A History of the South,* 93

in the event of a future war. New England's sentiment was split. Her manufacturers wanted a new deterrence tariff, but her legacy maritime and commerce interests were opposed. New York was also split with the city's commerce interests opposed and the state's manufacturers in favor. Thus, protective tariff support did not fall as much along geographic lines as it later would. Finally, those wanting to pay-off the national debt accumulated during the War of 1812 also argued for higher tariffs.[37]

The result was the Tariff of 1816, the first designed specifically to protect domestic manufacturers. It put heavy duties on targeted industries such as cotton textiles, iron, and wool. Some items had two types of tariffs: *ad valorem* and *specific duty*. Cotton goods, for example, had a 25% *ad valorem* fee. At the same time cotton goods costing less that 25-cents per yard were charged a specific fee of 6.25-cents per yard. The same structure applied to woolens. Thus, when prices dropped below 25-cents per yard the specific fee caused the tariff to rise above 25%. A 20-cent per yard price, for example, translated to a 31% tariff $[(6.25/20) = 31\%]$. Consequently, even though Britain's improving manufacturing technology led to sharp price reductions for coarse goods, the 6.25-cents per yard fee became a prohibitive tariff when they tried to sell such goods into the American market. The new tariff was set to expire in four years because it was only meant to give domestic manufacturers a limited time to improve their production efficiency.[38]

Although the 1816 Tariff had merits, its purpose was not to maximize government income but to optimize profits for targeted industries. It thereby became a new platform for crony-capitalism that would corrupt the legislative process for over a hundred years. It was seldom eclipsed as a crony tool until superseded by the income tax in the twentieth century. It enabled Federal politicians

---

[37] Hubert H. Bancroft, Ed. *The Great Republic by Master Historians: Volume III*, Available: https://tinyurl.com/y9ermtwr [Accessed: May 3, 2020]; William Fowler, *The Sectional Controversy*, 89

[38] F. W. Taussig, *A Tariff History of the United States*, 29-30

to offer profit optimization to well-connected industries in exchange for campaign donations, notwithstanding that it transferred wealth from the masses to the industrial centers. Consequently, tariff protection became as addictive as a barbiturate to those who benefitted. They increasingly craved more protection. By reducing imports, however, higher tariffs caused lower exports, most of which came from the South as explained in chapter one. As tariff scholar Douglas Irwin put it, "Congress was not far sighted in shaping the future path of the economy [with tariff policy] but simply reacted to the political pressures that it faced." Those pressures would increasingly come from Northern industrial interests.[39]

Consequently, the 1816 Tariff did not expire in 1820. Congress extended it temporarily while working to pass even higher tariffs. The first effort was the 1820 Baldwin Bill, which passed the House to increase general rates by five percent, with even higher increases on wool cloth, finished clothing, iron and hemp. The South, however, would no longer support more deterrence tariff increases for three reasons. First, the government had no urgent need for additional revenue. Second, there was no longer a lingering threat of war, which would necessitate that strategic goods be manufactured domestically. Third, there was likewise no immediate prospect of an import surge. Although the Baldwin Bill passed the House 91-78 in was tabled in the Senate by a 22-21 vote, with all 14 Southern senators voting to table. Nonetheless, many protective rates remained in force until a new bill passed both chambers in 1824.

The sectional differences that hardened during the early 1820s would remain in force until Woodrow Wilson became President in 1913. Southerners had no chance of defeating higher tariffs in the

---

[39] Douglas Irwin, *Clashing Over Commerce: A History of U. S. Trade Policy*, 130

Senator Henry Clay

House due to their lower population and two-fifths slave exclusion. Consequently, the South would try to retain a slave-state-to-free-state parity in the Senate in order to block higher tariffs. Even with parity, some slave states such as Henry Clay's Kentucky favored tariff protection.

During the 1820s the rapidly growing Midwest's trade interests were not so well defined as were those of the traditional North or South. Geographically the region would remain mostly isolated from foreign commerce until the railroads started to come of age in the 1840s. As it was, neither the North nor South could maintain a majority in both congressional chambers. Consequently, Midwestern congressmen and senators became the balance of power on tariff policy.

Eventually the North would win the Midwest's loyalty for three reasons. First, most of the railroads connected the region to Eastern ports above the Mason Dixon line. They would become more important transportation facilities than Mississippi River steamboats, which had previously connected the Midwest economically to the South. Second, some states North of the Ohio River would become important producers of products such as wool that could benefit from protective tariffs. Unlike Southern cotton farmers, America's Midwest was not the World's low-cost wool producer. Thus, the region's growers needed deterrence tariffs if they were to prosper. Third, Midwesterners favored Federal public works spending on projects such as canals, roads, and Great Lakes harbors. Funds for the projects came almost entirely from tariff collections above the normal needs of the Central Government.[40]

Geographic regions disclosed their true interests during the debates over the 1824 Tariff. The bill's two hundred and sixty itemized articles revealed a decided protectionist lobby influence. Such extensive itemization underscored growing crony capitalism. The bill's chief proponent, Henry Clay, wanted the Federal Government to bolster the economy by promoting manufacturing industries and establishing a second national banking system. He argued that his program, which he termed the American System, would reduce America's dependence on foreign markets by creating a strong domestic market through high protective tariffs. Instead of selling cotton to Europe to be made into cloth resold to American consumers, Clay envisioned planters selling cotton to the emergent American textile makers who would use American workers to produce the finished goods for domestic consumers. Surplus tariff revenues would fund the public works projects, then known as "internal improvements," that were too speculative for the individual states. Such Federal projects would be especially welcome in the newer states having only modest legacy infrastructure and small taxable bases. Given Kentucky's location and terrain he particularly wanted such works to include roads, bridges, and canals to provide a national transportation network.[41]

Southerners had two objections. First, higher tariffs discouraged exports of such goods as cotton and tobacco, as explained in chapter one. Moreover, the domestic market for such goods among American finished goods suppliers was small in comparison to the export market. Domestic cotton textile manufacturers consumed less than 20% of the South's cotton feedstock. Second, higher tariffs increased prices to consumers regardless of whether the items were purchased as imports or from

---

[40] *Ibid.*, 139, 157

[41] *Ibid.*, 142-43; William K. Bolt, "The Tariff in the Age of Jackson." (PhD diss., University of Tennessee, 2010) , 140

American suppliers. Thus, high tariffs hit the South a double blow; they tended to cause as a drop in the price of her agricultural products (or a decline in the quantity that overseas buyers could purchase) while simultaneously increasing the price of manufactured goods.[42]

Consequently, South Carolina's Robert Hayne addressed the Senate:

> I take this occasion to declare that we [the South] shall feel ourselves justified in embracing the very first opportunity of repealing all such laws as may be passed for the promotion of these [import protected] objects. Whatever interests may grow up under this bill, and whatever capital may be invested, I wish it to be distinctly understood that we will not hold ourselves bound to maintain the system; and if capitalists will, in the face of our protests and in defiance of our solemn warnings, invest their fortunes in pursuits made profitable at our expense, on their own heads be the consequences of their folly![43]

After the bill narrowly passed the House in April 1824 the Senate reduced some rates and passed an amended bill 25-to-21 with all fourteen Southern senators voting nay. President James Monroe signed it as the Tariff Act of 1824. It increased average rates on dutiable items from 38% to 42%.[44]

That same year, John Quincy Adams, son of America's second President, was himself elected President and served from 1825 to 1829. Since protective tariffs became increasingly popular in his home state of Massachusetts after the War of 1812, he wanted yet another tariff act during his administration to provide even more protection. The result was the 1828 Tariff, which became known as the Tariff of Abominations for two reasons. First, by 1832 it caused

---

[42] Douglas Irwin, *Clashing Over Commerce: A History of U. S. Trade Policy*, 145

[43] Edward Stanwood, *American Tariff Controversies of the Nineteenth Century*, (Boston: Houghton-Mifflin, 1903), 236

[44] Douglas Irwin, *Clashing Over Commerce: A History of U. S. Trade Policy*, 145

the average collection rate on dutiable items to rise to 62%. Second, it had a collusive structure designed to satisfy producers of raw materials and finished goods simultaneously despite their normally conflicting interests, as explained below.

Although finished goods manufacturers normally want imported raw materials to be duty-free, they simultaneously want their manufactured goods to be tariff protected. New England's woolen textile makers were one example. They wanted to import wool feedstock because it was cheaper than domestically produced wool. In contrast domestic sheep herders wanted protection from wool imports. As a result, the 1824 Tariff raised the rate on raw wool from 15% to 30% but only hiked the rate of woolen finished goods, such as carpets and blankets, from 25% to 33%. In 1827 the two sides met at a conference in Harrisburg, Pennsylvania where they colluded.

Under the presumed leadership of New York Senator and future President Martin Van Buren, tariff opponents planned to defeat any new initiative by crafting a bill that would increase the costs of raw materials but provide little relief for the manufacturers that transform such materials into finished goods. A House committee released such a bill in March 1828. It hiked rates on raw wool from 30% to 50% without changing the duties on finished woolen goods. Tariff opponents reasoned that such a bill would never pass since it would be rejected by the manufacturing lobby in the Senate because of its unfairness to woolen goods manufacturers.

If the strategy were to succeed, all attempts to amend the bill in the Senate had to be defeated. One such amendment raised the rate on finished woolen goods to 45% with an additional hike the following year to 50%. When it came to a vote, Senator Van Buren revealed his true colors and voted yea when tariff opponents had expected him to vote nay. Had he voted nay the amendment would have failed because Vice President John C. Calhoun was expecting to break the tie with a nay vote. After Van Buren's surprise approval vote, the Senate passed six more similar amendments. As a result, a joint House-Senate committee reshaped the bill to provide heavy tariff protection for *both* manufacturers and raw material suppliers.

Even President Adams recognized the excesses, but reluctantly signed the bill in May 1828. Southerners derived no benefit. Arguably, they might even have suggested that cotton growers were entitled to a subsidy to be paid from the tariffs collected. That way both the North *and* South would obtain at least some benefit.[45]

The Southern response took the form of the *South Carolina Exposition and Protest* published in December 1828 and written anonymously by Vice President Calhoun. He challenged the very right of Congress to pass tariffs for protection. The Constitution authorizes tariffs "as a tax power for the sole purpose of revenue; a power . . . essentially different than that of imposing protective or prohibitory duties. The two are incompatible. We [the South] cultivate certain staples for the supply of the general World; and they [the North] manufacture almost exclusively for the home market. Their object in the tariff is to keep down foreign competition, in order to obtain a monopoly of the domestic market. The effect on us is to compel us to purchase at a higher price, both what we purchase from them and from others, without receiving a corresponding increase of price for what we sell."

Calhoun's remarks were valid, especially for South Carolina. The Palmetto State was one of the oldest of cotton-growing states. Her plantations were the first to experience declining productivity. Lands in Alabama and Mississippi were more productive. Therefore, South Carolina cotton grower profitability was more sensitive to price. If, for example, a thousand-acre Alabama plantation could grow 25% more cotton than a thousand-acre South Carolina plantation, the difference showed up in the value of the farm as well as the profitability of the crop at harvest.

But Calhoun's analysis extends beyond conflicting economics. He perceived Northern dominance of tariff policy as symptomatic of a more fundamental challenge to minority rights and freedom.

---

[45] *Ibid.*, 147-152, 154; William K. Bolt, "The Tariff in the Age of Jackson." (PhD diss., University of Tennessee, 2010), 372

"No government based on the naked principle that the majority ought to govern . . . ever preserved its liberty for even a single generation. The history of all has been the same: injustice, violence and anarchy, succeeded by government of one or a few   . . . An unchecked majority is a despotism—and government is free . . . in proportion to the number . . . of checks by which its powers are controlled."

John C. Calhoun

Next he paves the way for Nullification and Secession. The delegated powers of the Constitution are the initial check. "All others are expressly reserved to the states and the people." The Central Government, he argued, could not be the judge of the limits of its own powers. "The right of judgement in such cases is an essential attribute of the sovereignty . . . of the states [which] clearly implies a veto . . . on the action of the Central Government."

Calhoun argued that the Constitution created "two distinct and independent sovereignties" leaving a state the right to interpose its sovereignty to nullify a Federal law which it believed violated the Federal Compact. When opponents argued that there was no power of interposition found in the Constitution, Calhoun replied that there was also no place in the Constitution where the Supreme Court was given the power to rule on the constitutionality of laws passed by Congress, or the state legislatures. The right of state interposition—just like the Supreme Court's privilege of judicial review that John Marshall invoked in 1803—rested on *inference*. South Carolina, or any of the other agreeing parties to the constitutional compact, would never have surrendered their sovereignty and entered the Federal Union if they had been required to relinquish that right. Whether the Federal

Government would honor Calhoun's claim—or revert to Marshall's—would remain a key question until after the 1832 Presidential election.

Meanwhile, Andrew Jackson took the White House away from John Quincy Adams in 1828. Although tariff legislation came up in 1832 when Jackson was seeking re-election, "Old Hickory" and opponent Henry Clay both regarded it as secondary to Jackson's intent to deny the Second Bank of the United States a renewal of its national charter. Nonetheless, when a July 1832 tariff modestly reduced the rates of the abominable tariff, South Carolina wanted deeper cuts. After the state completed its elections in October her new legislature held a special session that authorized a convention to formulate a new tariff initiative. On November 24, 1832 the convention passed an Ordinance of Nullification declaring the Tariffs of 1828 and 1832 unconstitutional, and thereby null and void. The ordinance forbade the collection of import taxes on foreign goods within the state after February 1, 1833. The state warned that any military action to force collection might cause South Carolina to secede from the Union and form a separate government.

Suddenly, tariffs were back in the limelight. President Jackson responded aggressively. First, he asked that Congress provide a Force Bill authorizing him to use military force against South Carolina if she refused to comply with Federal tariff laws. Second, he recommended a gradual reduction in the tariff over a number of years after the Federal debt was retired in 1833. As Congress pondered the matters, sympathy for South Carolina's viewpoint increased, although it remained a minority. Consequently, Jackson could not get his Force Bill passed without another compromise tariff bill. While Congress remained in session, South Carolina changed the 1 February deadline for ending tariff collections within its borders to 4 March.

Into the breach stepped defeated presidential candidate Henry Clay, as the Great Compromiser. He successfully crafted and passed a bill that would gradually reduce tariffs bi-annually over the next nine years, culminating with a sharp drop in the ninth year to reduce rates to the 1816 level. On March 1, 1833, both the Force Bill and Clay's tariff became law. Ten days later, South Carolina rescinded her Nullification Ordinance, but also nullified Jackson's Force Act. As a principle, therefore, the state never denounced the legitimacy of nullification.[46]

Since the 1833 compromise tariff promised bi-annual reductions for the next nine years, angry passions subsided. Nevertheless, it resulted in three long-term consequences. First, Northern industrialists and Southern agriculturalists would continue to be at odds over tariffs well into the twentieth century. Second, growth of the mostly agricultural Midwestern slave-free states would cause Northern industrial states to substitute anti-slavery rhetoric as a proxy for pro-tariff and anti-Southern arguments. The implied morality of such rhetoric was intended to bring the Midwest into an alliance with the North and isolate the South politically. Third, after the steep tariff hikes of the 1820s, Southerners realized that the North would use a simple majority vote to impose their policies on the Federal Government regardless Southern concerns. If Southerners evolved into a perpetual minority, nullification and secession may become their only defense.

---

[46] H. W. Brands, *Andrew Jackson: His Life and Times,* (New York: Doubleday, 2005), 440-41; Lucas Kelley, "The Nullification Crisis," *Virginia Tech: Essential Civil War Curriculum*, Available: https:/tinyurl.com/yangkhy9 , [Accessed: May 6, 2020]; Douglas Irwin, *Clashing Over Commerce: A History of U. S. Trade Policy*, 280, 337

CHAPTER 4: SLAVERY AS PROXY

THE 1820 MISSOURI COMPROMISE is often misrepresented as the North's first noble effort to confine slavery in the South. In reality, it was also a convenient proxy issue having a high ethical tone to disguise Northern intent to secure economic hegemony. As H. L. Mencken put it, "When somebody says it's not about the money, it's about the money." Significantly, the Compromise passed the same year that Northerners failed to augment the Tariff of 1816 with more protections in the Baldwin Bill. They reasoned, probably correctly, that any agricultural society based upon slavery would have an export economy and therefore oppose protective tariffs.

Historians Commager and Morison concluded that Missouri's 1819 statehood petition "was discussed and agitated—not as a moral question but as one of sectional power and prestige;" Regarding Northern deception, historian William Hesseltine wrote, "The Missouri question involved a constitutional problem of the nature of the States, but more deeply it involved the economic well-being of the respective sections. Thomas Jefferson . . . declared that the Federalists [Missouri slave-state opponents] had raised the question as a party trick. They had sought to divide the people geographically and had taken advantage of the virtuous feeling of the people on the matter of slavery. The trick served them well, for from that time slavery was never absent from national politics." According to historian Thomas Fleming, Jefferson concluded that "restricting the spread of slavery would not free a single person. It was a pseudo morality, a feel-good policy motivated more by hatred of Southerners than by concern for slaves."[47]

For thirty-three years between the 1787 Constitutional convention and Missouri statehood in 1820, the Mason-Dixon line along Pennsylvania's southern border and the Ohio River had been considered the geographic break between the free and slave states. About two-thirds of Missouri lay north of the mouth of the Ohio River on the state's eastern border but the state was also almost entirely South of the Mason-Dixon line. In 1787 America's free-to-slave state population split was about even, but by 1820 the free states had 54% of the population. Additionally, the two-fifths exclusion of slave population gave the free states 105 House members compared to only 81 for the slave states. Southerners increasingly realized that their power involving tariffs was generally limited to blocking unfair bills in the Senate thereby making Senate parity a crucial goal.[48]

Henry Clay took the lead in shaping an 1820 compromise that would last for thirty years. First, Missouri's admission as a slave state would be offset by Maine's admission as a free state. Although Maine had previously been a part of Massachusetts, the Bay State legislature authorized Maine to apply for independent statehood. After Missouri and Maine were admitted, America would have twenty-four states evenly divided between free and slave. Second, all future states north of Missouri's southern border could only join the Union as free states. At the time written the provision would apply only to states carved out of the Louisiana Territory because Texas, Oregon Territory and the Mexican Cession were not yet part of America. Thus, when the compromise was passed, the South had good prospects for gaining new states in Florida and Arkansas,

[47] Morison and Commager *The Growth of the American Republic: Volume 1*, 443; William B. Hesseltine, *A History of the South: 1607-1935*, 211, 216; Thomas Fleming, *A Disease of the Public Mind*, 94

[48] Morison and Commager *The Growth of the American Republic: Volume 1*, 442

whereas the North could likely form states out of Michigan, Wisconsin, Iowa, Minnesota and the Great Plains. Until 1850 each new free state admitted was basically paired with a new slave state thereby maintaining a power balance in the Senate. Due to faster population growth, however, by 1850 the free states had 147 congressmen compared to only 90 in the slave states.[49]

Although many Northern politicians welcomed slavery as an indirect way for attacking Southern economic interests, a minority were genuinely offended by the immorality of the practice and their numbers would grow as the topic slowly came to dominate the national discourse. In March 1820, future President John Quincy Adams even stated that he preferred disunion over keeping Massachusetts in the United States:

> The impression produced upon my mind by the progress of this discussion . . . is that the bargain between freedom and slavery contained in the Constitution . . . is morally and politically vicious. . . I favor this Missouri Compromise, believing it all that could be effected under the present Constitution, and from an extreme unwillingness to put the Union at hazard.

> But perhaps it would have been wiser . . . to have persisted in the restriction upon Missouri, till it should have terminated in a convention [of states] to revise and amend the Constitution. This would have produced a new Union of thirteen or fourteen states unpolluted with slavery, with a great and glorious object to effect, namely rallying to their standard the other states by the universal emancipation of their slaves. If the Union is to be dissolved, slavery is precisely the question on which it ought to break.[50]

---

[49] Hanes Walton, Sherman Puckett, Donald Deskins, *The African American Electorate: A Statistical History, Volume 1*, (Thousand Oaks, Ca.: SAGE Publishing, 2012), 106

[50] Herbert Agar, *The Price of Union*, (Boston: Houghton Mifflin, 1966), 205

With only six years left in his eighty-three-year life, Thomas Jefferson also gained sad insight after Northerners resorted to virtue-signaling over slavery as a way to attain economic dominance. In an 1820 letter to a friend about Missouri statehood he wrote, "This momentous question, like a fire bell in the night, awakened and filled me with terror. I considered it at once as the knell of the Union." Regarding slavery he continued, "I can say with conscious truth that there is not a man on earth who would not sacrifice more than I would to relieve us from this heavy reproach, in any practical way. . . But, as it is, we have a wolf by the ears, and we can neither hold him, or, safely let him go. Justice is on one scale and self-preservation on the other."[51]

John Quincy Adams

After slavery entered the political discourse as an indirect way of attacking Southern economic interests, sincere abolitionists also became more militant. Previous anti-slavery movements had focused on gradual or conditional emancipation. After the American Revolution Northern states began slowly emancipating slaves. New York was the biggest example. When slaves comprised less than 4% of her population the state passed a 1798 law declaring that all female slave children born after July 3, 1799 would be granted freedom in 1824 whereas male slave children would be freed in 1827. Until then they would be the property of their mother's owner. Less than 1% of the state's people

---

[51] H. W. Brands, *Heirs of the Founders*, 86-87

were slaves when the servitude periods ended between 1824 to 1827.

Conditional emancipation took the form of efforts to colonize black volunteers in Africa or elsewhere. One proponent was the African Colonization Society formed in 1816 by prominent Virginians. In time it was endorsed by five Southern legislatures and would include among its members Presidents Jefferson, Madison and Monroe as well as Kentucky's Senator Henry Clay. In 1822 the Society had established an African colony, which later became the independent country of Liberia. By 1860 six-thousand American slaves had relocated there.[52]

A little over two years after John C. Calhoun anonymously penned *The South Carolina Exposition and Protest* to the 1828 Tariff, William Lloyd Garrison founded *The Liberator*, a Boston abolitionist newspaper. It boldly advocated secession by featuring "No Union with Slaveholders" as a masthead slogan. Later in 1831 Nat Turner led a group of fellow Virginia slaves on a revolt that left about sixty whites, mostly women and children, massacred. In the early 1830s Garrison also helped organize the American Anti-Slavery Society. It was among the first of a steadily growing number of such organizations to demand an immediate and uncompensated end to slavery. Until then most anti-slavery movements, even in the North, focused on legislative action, an end to slave trade, and gradual emancipation. But Garrison was advocating that slaveholders free their slaves without any compensation notwithstanding that most were still obligated to repay the bank loans used to buy the slaves. By 1840 Garrison's society and similar

-----

[52] Columbia University, "Slavery and Emancipation in New York," Available: https://tinyurl.com/y8e7u7vv [Accessed: May 10, 2020]; Douglas Egerton, "Its Origin Is Not a Little Curious," *Journal of Free Men of the Early Republic*, v. 5, n.4 (Winter 1985): 463, 466; Jeffrey Rogers Hummel, *Emancipating Slaves, Enslaving Free Men,* (Chicago, Open Court, 1996), 20; Charles Adams, *When in the Course of Human Events,* (Lanham, Md.: Rowman & Littlefield, 2000), 133

organizations claimed 150,000 members, which was less than one percent of America's 17 million population.

The British boosted America's abolition movement in 1833 when Parliament abolished slavery in Britain's Western Hemisphere colonies to take effect in stages. Initially, slave children under age six were freed whereas those over age six were re-designated "apprentices" and continued to work much as before. As events transpired the apprenticeships ended in 1838. In addition to the value of the ex-slave's labor during apprenticeship, the British government paid slaveholders $110 million in compensation. The monetary amount averaged $132 for each man, woman and child slave, which compares to an average contemporary price for American slaves of $300. Specific American prices varied widely depending upon age, gender and location.[53]

Although the morality of British emancipation is undeniable, the economic benefits that abolitionists expected failed to materialize. Emeritus History Professor Pieter C. Emmer of the University of Leiden explains:

> The ending of . . . slavery should have produced progress, optimism, and gratefulness on all fronts. To many, however, the end of slavery in the Caribbean was a big disappointment. On average, the ex-slaves did not become yeomen farmers . . . as many had hoped. The abolitionists in Europe and North America . . . were dismayed. The pessimistic predictions of their adversaries about a dramatic decline in plantation output had proved all too real. Most abolitionists had not expected that so many of the freedmen would leave

---

[53] Samuel H. Williamson and Louis Cain, "Measuring Slavery in 2016 Dollars," MeasuringWorth.com, 2020, Available: https://tinyurl.com/gmclspn, [Accessed: May 11, 2020]; Julie Holcomb, "The Abolitionist Movement," *Virginia Tech: Essential Civil War Curriculum,* Available: https://tinyurl.com/ybzwmnsq [Accessed: May 11, 2020]; Jeffrey Rogers Hummel, *Emancipating Slaves, Enslaving Free Men,* 21; Morison and Commager *The Growth of the American Republic: Volume 1,* 556

the plantations or . . . fail to become the hard working, God-fearing peasantry that they had envisioned. Unwilling to admit that the fault lay with an unrealistic assessment on their own part, they attributed the blame to the planters as well as to the colonial and home governments.

Since the 1970s, however, the role of the planters in the plantation economies of the New World has been reinterpreted. The view that they were 'uneconomic', wasteful, and backward-looking autocratic rulers of a crumbling empire has been turned almost upside down. More recent studies . . . now portray the planters as highly efficient managers. . . New interpretations. . . confirm that the planters carefully tuned the purchase of slaves to their needs and were keen to avoid creating a wasteful mix of labour and capital. . . With slave prices rising, the planters also attempted to increase the natality, and decrease the mortality, of their slave populations by spending more plantation money on providing better food, housing, and medical care.[54]

Despite the poor results in the Caribbean, American abolitionists marched ahead. In 1831 they organized a postal campaign targeting Southern clergy, editors and politicians with thousands of copies of anti-slavery pamphlets. The campaign met a hostile reaction, North and South. A Charleston a mob broke into the post office, destroyed the literature and burned William Lloyd Garrison in effigy. A Boston mob that was looking for visiting British abolitionist George Thompson instead found Garrison and dragged him through the streets. Between 1835 and 1838 abolitionists sent Congress over 400,000 petitions, requesting the freedom of one, or more, slaves often located far from the petitioner's home. Among the most numerous were petitions to free the slaves in the District of

---

[54] Pieter Emmer, "The Big Disappointment: The Economic Consequences of the Abolition of Slavery in the Caribbean, 1833–1888," *Institute for Historical Research*, 2007, Available: https://tinyurl.com/ycwoe5ds [Accessed: May 11, 2020]

Columbia. Since there were only about 240 congressmen and 50 senators, the petitions created an impossible workload. As a result, Congress adopted various rules to ignore them so that work might proceed on other matters such as the 1837 financial crisis and ensuing depression. Among the abolitionists who fought such so-called gag rules was former President, and then-Congressman, John Quincy Adams. He finally got them repealed in 1844.[55]

Despite abolitionism's sanctimony, it only slowly became an effective proxy-weapon for Northern economic hegemony for two reasons. First, many Northerners were prejudiced against blacks. Since most abolitionists came from the elite classes and the clergy, they needed time to develop arguments that might show the common Northern man why it was in his interest to oppose slavery. Second, many Northerners benefitted from slavery. Among them were New England's cotton textile makers and the Northeastern commercial interests.

From the early nineteenth century many of the newly admitted states in the Midwest passed laws designed to minimize black immigration. Indiana and Ohio, for example, did not allow free blacks to enter their states nor to own property. Initially, Illinois required that newly arriving free blacks post a $1,000 bond. By 1853 even more exclusionary legislation effectively barred free blacks from moving into the state, which Abraham Lincoln never publicly condemned.

Neither were the Northeastern states free of racial prejudice. In 1833 Connecticut threw a Quaker schoolmistress in jail for integrating her private academy. In addition to the Boston mob attack on Garrison noted above, in 1834 New York rioters sacked the home of Lewis Tappen who funded several anti-slavery organizations. Similarly, Illinois abolitionist Elijah Lovejoy was

---

[55] Julie Holcomb, "The Abolitionist Movement," *Virginia Tech: Essential Civil War Curriculum,* Available: https://tinyurl.com/ybzwmnsq [Accessed: May 11, 2020]

publicly murdered in 1837. When French travelogue writer Alexis de Tocqueville toured America in 1830 he wrote, "race prejudice seems stronger in those states that have abolished slavery than in those states where it still exists, and in nowhere is it more intolerant than in those states where it was never known." Even if most Northerners might be persuaded to abolish black slavery in the South, they did not want blacks to migrate into the free states.[56]

Despite economic policy differences, many Northerners were also reluctant to oppose slavery because of their economic dependence upon the South. From 1830 to 1860 cotton consumed annually by Northern textile makers increased from 43 million pounds to 470 million, translating to a compound yearly growth rate of 8%. Similarly, cotton exported to Great Britain grew from 202 million pounds to 1.2 billion, yielding a compound growth rate of 3%. Over the same period cotton exports swelled from 41% to 58% of total American exports. By 1840 New England textile makers had 100,000 workers and they contributed two-thirds of the region's economic value-added within large-scale manufacturing. By 1860 Middlesex County Massachusetts alone had assessed property valuations that exceeded the entire state of South Carolina. Slavery scholar Ronald Baily concludes, "So strong was the need for cotton from the South that many of the leading Boston industrialists were active supporters of the slave owners and ardent anti-abolitionists before the Civil War."[57]

Furthermore, the South was dependent upon outside sources for nearly all manufactured items, either from imports or more often tariff-protected Northern suppliers. During its time in the Confederacy, the South had more railroad mileage than any country except the Federal Union. Yet when those states were in the Union,

---

[56] Jeffrey Rogers Hummel, *Emancipating Slaves, Enslaving Free Men*, 26-27; Charles Adams, *When in the Course of Human Events*, 130-31

[57] Ronald Bailey, "The Other Side of Slavery," *Agricultural History*, v.68, n.2, (Spring 1994): 37, 44, 49; J. G. Randall and David Donald, *The Civil War and Reconstruction*, 7

they were largely dependent upon tariff-protected Northern suppliers for railroad iron. In 1860 they had only 18,000 manufacturing plants employing 110,000 workers as compared to 110,000 factories and 1.3 million workers in the North. Among the manufactured items the South bought from the North were cotton cloth, boots and shoes, iron products, woolens, clothes, and hats.

America's firearms industry was headquartered in the Connecticut River Valley and shipbuilding was centered in the Northeast. The South had no gunpowder-making plants. New York banks and factors financed the cotton crop annually with seed money and loans collateralized by Southern land and slave property. Uncompensated emancipation would leave such loans vulnerable to default. Cotton plantations were also dependent upon corn and pork from the states North of the Ohio River. Notwithstanding Southern slavery, most Northerners so valued the economic benefits of the Union that Garrison's *Liberator* newspaper never had a circulation of more than 3,000.[58]

Nevertheless, by switching the narrative of sectional differences from economics to slavery, Northerners deceptively gained the moral high ground and increasingly condemned Southerners as depraved. Historian Edmund Wilson observed that rhetorical "exploitation of the wickedness of the planters became later a form of propaganda like the alleged German atrocities in Belgium at the start of the First World War. . . [Slavery] supplied the militant Union North with the rabble rousing moral issue which is necessary in every modern war to make the conflict appear as a melodrama." Such assaults provoked some Southerners to respond with ill-conceived arguments defending slavery. In 1844 the Methodist Church split into Northern and Southern branches. The next year

---

[58] Shelby Foote, *The Civil War: A Narrative, Volume 1*, (New York: Random House, 1957), 60; J. G. Randall and David Donald, *The Civil War and Reconstruction*, 23; Thomas Kettell, *Southern Wealth and Northern Profits*, (New York: George & John Wood, 1860), 59

the Baptists divided, leaving the two largest protestant denominations separated along geographic lines. Although Presbyterians remained unified a little longer it became increasingly clear that the institutions that provided national unity were breaking down.[59]

President James Buchanan

The great flaw of American abolitionism as it evolved toward demands of immediate and uncompensated emancipation was the fantasy that, if achieved, the goal would have no significant adverse consequences. Yet, there would obviously be at least two. First, abrupt emancipation would bankrupt the slaveowners who were often ultimately in debt to Northern bankers. Second, it would throw millions of ex-slaves out of work, suddenly requiring them to care for themselves in a broken economy caused by plantation bankruptcies. That was, in fact, almost precisely what happened after the Civil War. Emancipation impoverished the entire region, black and white. Such results make a mockery of the pious initiatives by antebellum abolitionists demanding abrupt and uncompensated emancipation.

On the eve of secession in December 1860 President James Buchanan denounced abolitionists. Although he argued that the Southern states had no right to secede over the results of a presidential election, he also condemned abolitionists for

---

[59] Jeffrey Rogers Hummel, *Emancipating Slaves, Enslaving Free Men*, 24; Edmund Wilson, *Patriotic Gore* (New York: W. W. Norton, 1962), xvi

vituperative agitation. "It cannot be denied that for five and twenty years the agitation at the North against slavery has been incessant. . . This agitation has ever since been continued by the public press, by the proceedings of State and county conventions and by abolition sermons and lectures. The time of Congress has been occupied in violent speeches on this never-ending subject, and appeals, in pamphlet and other forms, indorsed by distinguished names, have been sent forth from this central point and spread broadcast over the Union." Next he criticized such activism for recklessly ignoring the constitutional rights of the states. "As sovereign States, [the slave states] are responsible before God and the world for the slavery existing among them. For this the people of the North are not more responsible and have no more right to interfere than with similar institutions in Russia or Brazil."[60]

The abolition movement also had a conservative wing, preferring to call themselves anti-slavery men. Like Lincoln, they wanted to abide the constitution. They saw the economic folly of immediate and uncompensated emancipation and concluded that attempts to achieve it would "roll a wave of blood across the land," as Charles Finney put it. Among them were Brown University president Francis Wayland. He warned the left wing that their agitation made open discussion impossible. Ralph Waldo Emerson took a similar position. Even some on the left finally realized their demands were unrealistic. One was Theodore Weld who had authored a book on the evils of Southern slavery with carefully documented eye-witness accounts of his own and others. After watching Southerners respond in rage to sarcastic and pious attacks, he understood that extreme demands and rhetoric would fail. In an 1844 speech he asked his audience if they really believed America could be changed

---

[60] James Buchanan, "Fourth Annual Message to Congress," (December 3, 1860), Available: https://tinyurl.com/ycjbypq2 [Accessed: May 14, 2020]; Abraham Lincoln, "First Inaugural Address," (March 4, 1861) Available: https://tinyurl.com/y9ac6tp5 [Accessed: July, 2020]

by calling slaveholders vicious names. His answer was "no." Like many of the right wing, he left the movement.[61]

As everyone knows, and shall be examined in a later chapter, the anti-slavery forces would win. They would eventually attract the Northern common man by promising to reserve new lands for whites. Moreover, they would shift their arguments from facts and statistics to melodramatic narratives about slavery and fugitive slaves. But first, the political spotlight would again shift to tariffs in the early and mid 1840s.

---

[61] Morison and Commager *The Growth of the American Republic: Volume 1*, 559-60; Thomas Fleming, *A Disease of the Public Mind*, 135-36

CHAPTER 5: BREACHED AND RESTORED TARIFFS

AS EXPLAINED IN chapter three, Henry Clay led the 1833 compromise tariff bill that ended the South Carolina Nullification Crisis. For Northern manufacturers it ensured considerable protection for nine years with two sharp drops in the tenth year to a targeted revenue tariff of 20%, which was assumed to be enough to finance the operations of the Federal Government. The starting point for the rate cuts were the duties itemized in the high 1832 Tariff.

All 1832 rates above 20% were to be reduced in four biannual cuts, each representing one tenth of the difference between the 20% goal for July 1, 1842 and the 1832 rate. Thus, by 1840 four-tenths of the excess over 20% would be gone. Then on January 1, 1842 half of the remaining excess would be taken off, followed by another cut for the final half six months later. The ten-year delay for the final steep cuts was intended to give domestic manufacturers time to adjust even though some of the last cuts would be abrupt. Rolled iron bars, for example, were protected by a 95% tariff in 1832 and even as late as the start of the tenth year stood at 65%. They would have to drop the final 45% in the first six months of 1842. As a result, when the calendar approached the tenth year the tariff protection lobby reneged.[62]

---

[62] Douglas Irwin, *Clashing Over Commerce: A History of U. S. Trade Policy*, Kindle Locations: 3708-3724; F. W. Taussig, *A Tariff History of the United States*, 98

The result was the Black Tariff. As it happened, the targeted 20% rate remained in force only two months, July and August 1842. Congress quickly sent two bills to President John Tyler during those months. Both were misrepresented as revenue tariffs. In reality they included major protectionist features. Tyler vetoed both and was banished from the Whig Party, which was strongly pro-tariff. Nonetheless, he had two good reasons for his vetoes.

First, both tariff bills broke faith with the 1833 Compromise Tariff that mandated 20% rates by mid-1842. Second, the expiring 1833 Act included a provision that would restrict Federal Government access to funds from public land sales if 1842 tariffs did not drop to 20%, as scheduled. Tyler needed access to recent land sale proceeds in order to avoid a big budget deficit. On a third late August try, Congress finally passed a tariff bill that enabled the government to use land sale funds and Tyler reluctantly signed it. The resultant Black Tariff increased the average rates from 26% to 37% and doubled the duties on protected items. It squeaked by on a margin of 104-to-103 in the House and 24-to-23 in the Senate.

Although an obvious breach of faith, the 1842 Black Tariff passed for two reasons. First, the steep and abrupt cuts scheduled for the first half of 1842 were too much for the protected industries. They could not adapt quickly enough. Even though they had almost ten years to prepare, they neglected their responsibility. Second, the 1842 economy was weak due to the depression that followed the 1837 Financial Panic. Federal revenues dropped from $48 million in 1836 to $20 million in 1842. Nearly 85% of the $28 million drop was caused by a decline in the sales of Federal lands. Land speculation virtually ended after the Second Bank of the United States lost its charter in 1836 forcing many unprepared speculators to paydown their loans. Simultaneously, state governments started floating large borrowings in order to fund public works, particularly in the Midwest. Many projects were overly ambitious and collapsed, leading to further bank failures in 1839. By 1841 the Federal

Government was operating with a $10 million annual deficit and a projected $5 million deficit for 1842.[63]

President John Tyler

Since they had received only gradual and limited tariff cuts under the 1833 Compromise Tariff, Southerners were furious. John C. Calhoun complained, "We have patiently waited the nine years of slow reduction, and resisted every attempt to make changes . . . in our favor . . . And now . . . when it is our turn to enjoy the benefits, they who called on us to adhere to the [1833 Act] . . . coolly and openly violate every provision in our favor." Similarly, Virginia's Representative John Jones said, "while the South had to bear the burdens of the arrangements, it tamely and quietly submitted to the consequences. . . Now, when we are to reap the advantages of the compromise act . . . we see . . .the very party who enacted the law have come forward and declared that they will not execute the promises nor discharge the obligation there imposed."[64]

After Democrats won the 1842 midterm elections, the House Ways and Means Committee proposed a bill that would establish new rates. They would be above the 20% target level set by the 1833 Act but below those of the Black Tariff. Since the Midwest had been

---

[63] "U. S. Federal Government Revenues 1790-Present: 1975," *CRS Report of Congress*, Available: https://tinyurl.com/ybvbxoor [Accessed: May 17, 2020]; Douglas Irwin, *Clashing Over Commerce: A History of U. S. Trade Policy*, Kindle Locations: 3708-3724

[64] Douglas Irwin, *Clashing Over Commerce: A History of U. S. Trade Policy*, Kindle Locations: 3744-3753

growing rapidly and producing surplus crops, high tariff opponents gained important allies in the region. Indiana, Illinois and Ohio were producing more grain and other foods than needed to supply domestic demand. Thus, their only options were to either wastefully destroy the surplus or sell it into the export market. Simultaneously, Britain was considering a repeal of its Corn Laws that had traditionally restricted grain imports into the U.K. Initially the Laws prohibited imports below a specified price but later imposed steep tariffs that also effectively blocked imports. Notwithstanding their 1842 midterm election gains, however, U.S. tariff reduction proponents didn't have enough votes to get a new bill through Congress. They'd have to hope for better results in the 1844 elections.

When the 1844 presidential race ended, Democrat James K. Polk narrowly beat Whig Henry Clay in the popular vote but won the electoral college decisively. As father of the American System, voters were well aware of Clay's pro-tariff stance, which Democrats targeted during the campaign. Despite Polk's slim popular vote margin Democrats won majorities in both chambers of Congress.

President Polk outlined his tariff policies during his first annual message to Congress in December 1845. Although he stressed that the 1842 Black Tariff violated the tariff-for-revenue principles of the 1833 Compromise, he conceded a need for some protective measures: "I am far from entertaining opinions unfriendly to manufactures. On the contrary, I desire to see them prosperous so far as they can be without imposing unequal burdens on other interests." He wanted a simplified tariff; one that would abolish specific duties and minimum valuations, replacing them with simple percentage rates. Days later Treasury Secretary Robert Walker revealed the Administration's plan. Walker argued that the prior complex protectionist schedules favored manufacturers over farmers, merchants, tradesmen, and the shipping industry and did little for laborers. Instead of nurturing prosperity, he explained, high domestic tariffs encouraged and perpetuated existing foreign trade barriers to the detriment of American exports.

Yet Walker did not endorse a single percentage for all items, as did the 20% target rate of the 1833 Tariff. He reasoned that some goods, such as luxuries, should bear more. As a result, his schedule included nine separate categories, A through I. Schedule A items, such as alcoholic beverages like brandy, would be taxed at 100%. Schedule B items, such as wine and fresh fruit, were to be taxed at 40%. A long list of products including ready-made clothing and raw tobacco were put in Schedule C and taxed at 30%. Other cotton textiles, such as cloth, were in Schedule D to be taxed at 25%. Items in Schedule E to be taxed at 20% included bacon, bananas and sawed timber. The next three categories were taxed at 15%, 10% and 5%. Products in the final class were duty free. Walker's schedules demonstrated how tariffs could be simplified when drafted by specialists dedicated to the good of the entire country instead of groups of disparate lobbyists concerned only with the interests of their clients. He pointedly avoided the complexity of combining percentage rates and conditional specific duty fees.

The House waited seven months after President Polk's annual message before voting on the bill because they first wanted to see if Britain would repeal her Corn Laws, which she did in June 1846. Her repeal made Walker's bill more attractive to Midwesterners hoping to export grain to the U.K. The House passed the Walker Bill 114-to-95 in July after getting coffee and tea put on the duty-free list, but a fierce Senate fight lay ahead. Pennsylvania and Connecticut Democrats were ready to vote nay due to their regional iron and textile interests. A tie vote seemed plausible. That put Vice President George Dallas of Pennsylvania under conflicting loyalties. Polk's agents intercepted one senator at a Washington train station before he left for a visit home. They took him to the White House where the President persuaded him to remain in town for the vote. After deciding that he would stay Party-loyal, Vice President Dallas was spared the need to make a tie-breaking vote when the Senate approved the bill 29-to-28 in late July 1846.

Afterward, President Polk wrote in his diary that the effort put into passing the legislation had given "rise to an immense struggle between the two great political parties. . . The capitalists and the monopolists have not surrendered the immense advantages which they possessed, and the enormous profits which they derived under the tariff of 1842, until after a . . . mighty struggle. This city has swarmed with them for weeks. They have spared no effort within their power to sway and control Congress, but all has proved to be unavailing and they have been at length vanquished. Their effort will now probably be to raise a panic . . . [among the public] so as to induce a repeal of the act." He was correct about the attempted repeal, but it failed.[65]

The Walker Tariff, which would remain in force for eleven years, was a big success. It dropped average rates from 34% in 1845 to 26% in 1848. Despite the lower rates, customs duties increased from $26 million in 1847 to $68 million ten years later. During the same period imports grew from $150 million to $360 million while exports increased from $155 million to $365 million. The value of cargos carried in U.S. flagged ships advanced from $250 million to $510 million. Each statistic grew at a compound annual rate of about 9%. The Gross Domestic Product similarly grew from $2.4 billion to $4.1 billion translating to a compound yearly increase of almost 6%.[66]

At the end of 1856 the Federal budget had been running surpluses for seven consecutive years. During that period the total accumulated revenues of $420 million exceeded expenses of $365

---

[65] Douglas Irwin, *Clashing Over Commerce: A History of U. S. Trade Policy*, Kindle locations: 3756-3852

[66] U. S. Department of Commerce, "Historical Statistics of the United States: Colonial Times to 1970: Part 2," (Washington: U. S. Government Printing Office, 1975), 761; MeasuringWorth.com, Available: https://tinyurl.com/zrmljld [Accessed: May 18, 2020]

million by 15%. As a result, Congress passed a new tariff bill in 1857, which President James Buchanan signed in March. The new lower tariff met little resistance because of then-applicable treasury rules. Specifically, accumulated budget surpluses were deposited in the Treasury in order to avoid tempting Congress to spend them. Since money sitting idly in Treasury vaults would also reduce the circulating money supply thereby slowing down the economy, commercial interests favored the bill. They wanted to get the Treasury money back in circulation. Most of the opponents were Pennsylvania iron producers and wool growers in New England and the Midwest who were focused on their own interests instead of the national economy.

The biggest conflict was between New England's woolen goods makers and the growers of raw wool. New England factories wanted unprocessed wool imports to be duty-free thereby lowering their manufacturing costs. That caused a big protest among Midwestern wool growers who informed the textile makers that such a tariff would drive them to ally with Southerners who wanted only minimal tariffs on nearly all items including woolen finished goods. In the end, wool growers remained disgruntled. Although the cut on iron products from 30% to 24% angered Pennsylvanians, the powerful railroad industry wanted better prices on quality rails. On average the 1857 Tariff cut the rate on dutiable items from 26% in 1856 to slightly under 20% in 1860, which was nearly the lowest point of the nineteenth century. The 1857 Tariff also continued to avoid specific duties and minimum valuations that were commonly abused to inflate the profits of domestic manufacturers.[67]

A month after the new tariff was enacted in July, the failure of the Ohio Life Insurance & Trust Company triggered an economic

---

[67] Kenneth Stampp, *America in 1857: A Nation on the Brink,* (New York: Oxford University Press, 1992), 19-22; U. S. Department of Commerce, "Historical Statistics of the United States: Colonial Times to 1970: Part 2," 1106; Douglas Irwin, *Clashing Over Commerce: A History of U. S. Trade Policy,* Kindle locations: 4150-4162

downturn. Although headquartered in Cincinnati, the company's biggest operation was its Wall Street bank. Instead of writing insurance, or even issuing banknotes, it took deposits from well-heeled New Yorkers and brokers. The deposits were offered to Midwestern commercial houses in exchange for allegedly gilt-edged collaterals, which included regional railroad bonds. The bank also functioned as agent for the state of Ohio and did considerable business with Ohio corporations.

A downturn in grain exports magnified the 1857 panic. After the Walker Tariff was adopted in 1846 Midwestern grain exports began to grow, prompting a regional economic boom. Export growth accelerated during the 1853-1856 Crimean War because European farmers had been diverted to military service, causing a decline in European grain production. After the war ended and the soldiers returned to their farms, however, European grain production increased. That caused American grain exports to decline, which triggered a collapse in the Midwestern economy and a steep decline in the value of its temporarily overbuilt railroads, which the Ohio Insurance Company had taken as collateral for its Wall Street bank loans.

After the bank announced that it could not pay its depositors, other Wall Street brokers began calling-in their loans often demanding payment in specie, which was in short supply. The financial panic segued into an economic slowdown. Tariff revenues declined from $69 million in 1857 to $54 million in 1860 while GDP only inched forward from $4.2 billion to $4.4 billion. Initially international trade dropped 16% from 1857 to 1858 but set new records by the end of 1860 because the South's exports continued to grow while the North's economy remained in the doldrums. In 1859 President James Buchanan concluded he needed higher tariffs to balance the budget. Perhaps because of loyalties to the iron makers of his native Pennsylvania, he even advocated renewed usage of specific tariffs and valuation minimums in addition to *ad valorem* rates. On the eve of the Civil War the stage was set for the biggest showdown battle on tariffs in fourteen years. After 1846, however, slavery moved back into the political spotlight.[68]

---

[68] U. S. Department of Commerce, "Historical Statistics of the United States: Colonial Times to 1970: Part 2," 1106, 1114; Kenneth Stampp, *America in 1857: A Nation on the Brink*, 221-22

CHAPTER 6: SLAVERY AND RACE

FROM 1840 TO 1860 America's population increased from about 17 million to 32 million while the number of slaves grew from 2.5 million to 4.0 million. The percent of total population represented by slaves declined slightly from 15% to 13%. At the beginning of the period the country had twenty-six states, evenly split between slave and free. Seven more states joined the Union but only Texas and Florida were slave states. Iowa, Wisconsin, Minnesota, California and Oregon joined as free states. The slave states lost parity in the Senate in 1850 and by 1860 were outnumbered 18-to-15. In 1840 free states had 135 congressmen as compared to 88 for the slave states. Ten years later free states had 147 congressmen compared to only 90 for the slave states. Simultaneously, America's boundaries leaped westward from the Missouri and Red rivers to the Pacific Ocean. The new lands included the 1845 Texas Annexation, 1846 Oregon Settlement and 1848 Mexican Cession. During the late 1840s and most of the 1850s, relative peace over tariffs left slavery and race to dominant politics by default.

After the 1803 Louisiana Purchase some Americans claimed the territory's western border was the Rio Grande River. But when he negotiated the 1819 treaty annexing Florida, President Monroe's Secretary of State, John Quincy Adams, drew the state of Louisiana's western border at the Sabine River. A few years later Mexico permitted Stephen Austin to take three-hundred American families into the region known as Texas beyond the Sabine and north of the Rio Grande, giving each family 4,000 acres. A decade later when about 20,000 Americans were living in Texas, Mexico decided to slow the migration because most Americans declined to become Roman Catholic and otherwise assimilate into Mexican culture. Consequently, Mexico City suspended unoccupied land grants in Texas and temporarily blocked additional migration. In 1836 American Texans revolted and won a peace treaty in May of that year. Although Texans declared independence, Mexico disputed the claim as well as the region's border. Texas argued her boundary was the Rio Grande whereas Mexico held that it was the Nueces River. The Rio Grande line gave Texas more than twice as much land.

Texas promptly asked to be annexed by the United States, but President Andrew Jackson urged that she wait until after a new President was elected later in 1836. After New York's Martin Van Buren moved into the White House in March 1837, however, he was reluctant to annex Texas. Consequently, Texas began to negotiate with Great Britain to mediate an agreement between Texas and Mexico. The British were amenable because mediated terms might work to the U.K.'s advantage. Under British protection, for example, Texas might become an independent source of cotton and could stand as a buffer state to restrain America's geographic and economic growth. Southerners objected to such intervention because it would weaken their region's cotton dominance and would block Southern ability to geographically expand. Therefore, President John Tyler, who served from March 1841 to March 1845, tried to acquire the Texas Republic. Initially he had quietly secured pledges for a two-thirds vote in the Senate as required to validate an international treaty. But free state senators backed out when they became worried that Texas annexation might result in a number of new slave states if Texas later decided to subdivide itself.

Toward the end of Tyler's Administration, James K. Polk became President-elect on a Manifest Destiny pledge to acquire Texas and settle a lingering boundary dispute with the British over Oregon

President James K. Polk

Territory. Tyler interpreted Polk's election as a mandate to acquire Texas. While Polk waited for his inauguration day, Tyler secured a joint congressional resolution authorizing Texas annexation, arguably circumventing the need for a two-thirds Senate vote. On his last full day in office Tyler sent a messenger to Texas with a version of the resolution that would admit Texas as a slave state and specified that her future borders would be settled in negotiations between the Federal Government and Mexico. A promptly informed Polk agreed to let the messenger continue. Texas voters formally accepted annexation on October 13, 1845.

When Mexico rejected Polk's ensuing border settlement offers, which included an attempt to buy California, the new President sent a military force under General Zachary Taylor to the Rio Grande. Upon arrival Taylor began building a fort near the mouth of the river early in 1846 thereby presuming that the Rio Grande—not the Nueces—was the true Texas border. His presence prompted an incident with Mexican forces who crossed the river and killed several American soldiers. As a result, America declared war on Mexico in May 1846. A month later Britain and America signed an Oregon border treaty, leaving Polk free to focus on Mexico, define Texas' borders, and acquire California.[69]

---

[69] Morison and Commager *The Growth of the American Republic: Volume 1*, 602-05,

Although Polk enlarged U.S. borders more than any President, many Northern politicians opposed his actions. One example was thirty-eight-year-old Illinois Congressman Abraham Lincoln who served one term from December 1847 to March 1849. Soon after taking his seat he demanded that Polk provide proof that General Taylor had not deliberately triggered the war by making an unprovoked attack on a Mexican village. The following month Lincoln voted for a resolution stating that the war was "unnecessarily and unconstitutionally begun by the President of the United States."[70]

The Mexican War lasted twenty-two months, ending in February 1848 with the Treaty of Guadalupe Hidalgo. Mexico ceded Texas with the Rio Grande as its border. It also gave-up the Mexican Cession, which included the future states of New Mexico, Arizona, California, Nevada and parts of other mountain states. The United States paid Mexico $15 million and assumed the unpaid debts of the acquired territories. Only a week before the treaty was signed, gold was discovered at Sutter's Mill on the American River in California, although word did not get out until later.[71]

Twelve weeks after the war started, Pennsylvania Congressman David Wilmot tried to derail it by attaching a rider to a $2 million funding bill requiring that slavery be prohibited in any territories acquired as a result of the war. Although the soon-named Wilmot Proviso is commonly misinterpreted as a moral weapon against slavery, it was really motivated by white supremacy. Specifically, Wilmot wanted to reserve the new territories for white families. "I make no war upon the South," he said when introducing the rider, "nor upon slavery in the South. I have no squeamish sensitiveness upon the subject of slavery, nor morbid sympathy for the slave. I

610-613; William B. Hesseltine, *A History of the South: 1607-1935*, 299-300, 303-04

[70] David Donald, *Lincoln,* (London: Jonathan Cape, 1995), 123-24

[71] Morison and Commager *The Growth of the American Republic: Volume 1,* 616

plead the cause of the rights of white freemen. I would preserve for free white labor a fair country, a rich inheritance, where the sons of toil, of my own race and own color, can live without the disgrace which association with negro slavery brings upon free labor." Although the Proviso passed the House it failed in the Senate.[72]

Notwithstanding Wilmot's admission that his Proviso was rooted in white supremacy instead of goodwill toward the slave, anti-slavery interests increasingly argued that its defeat in the Senate revealed the Southerner's depravity and his undue influence in the government. They came to two conclusions. First, they must end the South's parity power balance in the Senate. Second, they must change their political narrative to one of morality in the North versus immorality in the South thereby encouraging the public to ignore constitutional limits on majority power.

Consequently, they portrayed the South as a Slave Power, responsible for retarding the progress of the entire country in defense of an evil institution. For their part, the slave states realized that a future loss of Senate parity would leave them dependent upon strict interpretation of the constitution to limit the power of a simple majority which could otherwise rule tyrannically. Northerners would increasingly ignore their own revulsion to blacks and oppose Southern initiatives with strawman *ad hominin* attacks against the people of the entire region. One such leader, Edward Atkinson, would later classify all white Southerners as either arrogant planters or "poor white trash." Such arguments were not intended to persuade one's opponents. They were the kind which prepare men to kill one another. The time was not long past in the North—and still remained in parts of the South—when

---

[72] David Wilmot, "A Congressman "Pleads the Case of White Men"," *HERB: Resources for Teachers*, Available: https://tinyurl.com/y5fknbas [Accessed: May 21, 2020]

merely describing an aristocrat as a liar might cause the accused to respond with a challenge for a duel.[73]

The first emotional appeal by abolitionists to prompt Northern politicians into action and start them on the path to demagoguery was the plight of the runaway slave. Although writ large in the imaginations of year-2020 observers, the number of fugitive slaves were small. According to the 1860 census only 800 slaves escaped that year, down from 1,000 in 1850. Each figure represented three-tenths of one percent, or less, of the number of slaves. Additionally, most of the runaways never reached a free state or Canada. Moreover, since the population growth of free blacks in the North was slower than in the South, historians conclude that the annual number of fugitive slaves was lower than the census estimate. Historian James McPherson puts the figure at "perhaps" several hundred a year. That's because most of them were unable to get beyond the slave states before being recaptured.

If three hundred escaped annually, the cumulative number of fugitive slaves living in free states or Canada over the fifty-years from 1810 to 1860 may be estimated at 15,000 under the most generous assumptions. Given applicable life expectances and assuming the average fugitive ran away at age eighteen, it's likely they represented no more than four-tenths of one percent of the 1860 slave population that totaled four million.[74]

For nearly forty years the 1793 Fugitive Slave Act worked smoothly. In 1826, however, Pennsylvania passed a law making it a felony to forcibly remove any black from the state. The law was finally tested in 1837 when slavecatcher Edward Prigg took

---

[73] Ludwell Johnson, *Division and Reunion: 1848-1877,* (New York: Wiley, 1978), 12; Edward Atkinson, *Cheap Cotton by Free Labor,* (Boston: A. Williams & Company, 1861), 4

[74] U. S. Bureau of Census, 1860 *Census: Introduction,* Available: https://tinyurl.com/kwvkpbk; [Accessed: May 21, 2020], xvi; David M. Potter, *The Impending Crisis,* (New York: Harper Colophon, 1976), 136; James McPherson, *Battle Cry of Freedom,* (New York: Oxford, 1988), 79

runaway Margret Morgan back to Maryland where he intended to return her to the heirs of her deceased owner, John Ashmore. Five years earlier she had moved from Maryland to Pennsylvania where she had been living in virtual freedom ever since, although Ashmore had never officially set her free. Pennsylvania arrested Prigg for violating the state's 1826 Act and convicted him in 1839. He appealed to the United States Supreme Court on grounds that the Pennsylvania law could not supersede the 1793 Federal law, or the Fugitive Slave provisions contained in Article IV of the Constitution.

In the unanimous 1842 *Prigg v. Pennsylvania* decision the Court ruled the Pennsylvania law was illegal because the Constitution's supremacy clause trumped it, just as Prigg's lawyers had argued. However, it also ruled that the individual states need not help enforce the 1793 Act if state statutes prohibited cooperation. Thus, while a state could not arrest a slavecatcher for performing his work, it need not require that its enforcement apparatus help him. By 1850 nine free states had passed various statutes—known as personal liberty laws—designed to deny such cooperation and make it difficult for slavecatchers to capture and remove fugitive slaves.

Some of the laws were highly restrictive. They permitted local and state law enforcement to avoid helping the slavecatcher, denied him the use of jails for holding fugitives under Federal law, and required jury trials before removing suspected runaways from the state. Although the statistical impact of *Prigg* has never been quantified, slaveowners concluded that the 1793 Act could only be reliably enforced under Federal regulation, which would require a new law Federal law. Since free states had a decisive numerical advantage in the House and parity in the Senate, there was no chance that a new law would be adopted without a change in political circumstances, as shall be described.[75]

---

[75] J. G. Randall and David Donald, *The Civil War and Reconstruction*, 122n; William B.

General Zachery Taylor

Honoring a promise to be a one-term President, Polk did not seek reelection in 1848. His Democrat Party split when former President Martin Van Buren failed to get the nomination and ran as a candidate for the new Free-Soil Party on a platform to block the extension of slavery into Federal territories such as Kansas and Nebraska. The remaining Democrats nominated Michigan's Lewis Cass, a previous state governor and cabinet officer for Andrew Jackson. On the matter of slavery in the territories, Cass favored a local option principle that would permit the residents of a territory to decide for themselves by majority vote. Whig candidate General Zachary Taylor, who had never before even voted, opposed Cass and Van Buren. Since Taylor was a military hero in the recently victorious Mexican War and Cass's Party was split, Taylor won the election without saying much about his views. When Taylor took office in March 1849 the Mexican Cession was organized into military districts. Almost immediately the major issue was to decide which districts could become territories on the road to statehood and whether slavery would be allowed in such territories. Due to the Forty-Niner gold rush, California wanted to skip territorial status and promptly become a state. In only a few months San Francisco

Hesseltine, *A History of the South: 1607-1935*, 273; James McPherson, *Battle Cry of Freedom,* 79

had grown from a small village to a city of 20,000. Taylor's military governor scheduled a statehood constitutional convention in Monterey for September 1849, which was ratified by a 12,000-to-800 popular vote. Since most of the region's settlers were from free states, the state constitution outlawed slavery. Without waiting for congressional approval, California elected a governor and legislature, both scheduled to start operating in 1850.

By the time the Thirty-First Congress met for its first session in December 1849, California was clamoring for admission. Even though he owned many Louisiana slaves, Taylor thought California should be admitted as a free state given the 15-to-1vote margin noted above. As for New Mexico and Utah, Taylor proposed to organize them as territories without any reference to slavery. Such policies suggest that he was adopting Lewis Cass's territorial option principle, even though Southerners increasingly argued that it abrogated their constitutional right to take their slaves into any Federal territory because the territories were common to all Americans. The most extreme among such critics felt that application of Cass's territorial option might justify slave state secessions. Taylor left no doubt of his opinion when he told a group of visiting Georgia politicians that he would lead an army himself to put down any such regional secession. Since experienced politicians were not yet ready for intersectional warfare, Henry Clay once again fashioned a compromise with five provisions.

First, was immediate admission of California as a free state. Second, Utah and New Mexico were to be organized as territories without mention of slavery. Three, slave trade in Washington, D.C. was to end. Fourth, a new Fugitive Slave Law providing Federal provisions for enforcement had to be adopted. Fifth, was a requirement for Federal assumption of debts accumulated by Texas when she was an independent republic. Known as the Compromise of 1850 the plan gave occasion for the great Senate orators Clay, Webster and Calhoun to make farewell addresses.

In an aged and wavering voice Clay once again urged passionate devotion to the Union. Similarly, Daniel Webster spoke in favor of preserving the Union. Although abolitionists never forgave him, he used richer language to echo Clay's sentiments. Unlike Clay and Webster, whose regions where not threatened with marginalization, South Carolina's John C. Calhoun warned that the country could not remain united without additional guarantees to the South. Too feeble to speak for himself, Calhoun had Virginia Senator James Mason read his speech on March 2, 1850. "The cords that bind the States together" are snapping. Ten or more new free states might be carved out of the Federal territories remaining after 1850 but prospects for new slave states in the Southwest were minimal. The South must either grow, or wither. If she could not expand as the country expands, she could not stay in the Union.

While the bills were working through Congress, President Taylor died unexpectedly. New York's Millard Filmore assumed the Presidency in July 1850 and signed all the bills in September. In the South, the Democrat and Whig Parties lingered in name only as two successor groups vied for control. One was the Union Party led by three Georgians, Alexander Stephens, Robert Toombs and Howell Cobb. The other was a secessionist party led by Robert Rhett, John Quitman and William Yancey of South Carolina, Mississippi and Alabama, respectively. Although the Compromise provided a temporary peace, historian Ludwell Johnson concluded that it was ultimately fatal to Southern independence: "Northern conquest of the South in the early 1850s probably would have been impossible. In 1860 that was no longer true."[76]

Although the new Fugitive Slave Act angered abolitionists, most Northerners would likely have acquiesced but for several incidents inflamed by abolitionists. Only a month after Filmore signed the

---

[76] Morison and Commager *The Growth of the American Republic: Volume 1*, 621-28; Ludwell Johnson, *Division and Reunion*, 19; William B. Hesseltine, *A History of the South: 1607-1935*, 351-59; David Potter, *The Impending Crisis*, 56, 81

Act, abolitionist Theodore Parker and other Boston elites smuggled two slaves out of the country in October 1850 because agents were known to be travelling to the city to return them to Georgia. In November, Vermont passed a personal liberty law that made the Act unenforceable in the state. In April 1851, Federal authorities successfully enforced the law in Boston for the first time, but the security costs against mob interference amounted to $5,000. The attendant publicity fueled New England's animosity against the Act. Afterwards, the law was only once again enforced in Boston, which was three years later. Military force was required to control a Detroit mob attempting to interfere with a fugitive capture in October 1850. That same month a mob of 2,000 broke into a Syracuse jail to remove a fugitive salve. A year later Pennsylvania blacks murdered a slavecatcher. In March 1854 a Milwaukee mob broke into a jail to rescue an alleged fugitive.[77]

Acrimony over the Fugitive Slave Act prompted a forty-year-old housewife to propose that a Washington-based abolitionist weekly publish a twelve-week serial of a fictional anti-slavery story she would write. Fifteen months later, in June 1851, the *New Era* published the first episode of Harriet Beecher Stowe's *Uncle Tom's Cabin*. The story became so popular that Stowe was obliged to lengthen the serial from twelve to forty weeks. The following year it was published as a book and sold 300,000 copies before the end of 1852. In August of that year the first of numerous stage versions debuted. The book also sold well in Europe. A few Russian landowners claimed it motivated them to liberate their serfs. Leo Tolstoy pronounce it "one of the greatest productions of the human mind." Lord Palmerston, who would become British Prime Minister during America's Civil War, read it three times after having failed to pick up a single novel in the preceding three decades.

---

[77] David Potter, *The Impending Crisis*, 133-34

Stowe's husband was an abolitionist like her father and famous brother, clergyman Henry Ward Beecher. The month before Harriet proposed her serial to the *New Era*, Henry had published a pamphlet questioning Clay's 1850 Compromise and focused his objections on the Fugitive Slave Act. Nevertheless, Harriet actually knew little about slavery having only once visited a plantation in Kentucky. But she lived for years in Cincinnati where she was involved in the Underground Railroad. She also became acquainted with Ohio's Salmon P. Chase who would become a Republican Party leader, future Treasury Secretary under Lincoln and finally Supreme Court Chief Justice. After the Civil War she moved to Florida in 1866 where she purchased an orange grove plantation and endorsed brother Henry's opinion that it would be "unwise . . . to force negro suffrage upon the South."

Harriet Beecher Stowe

While her novel had sympathetic portrayals of a few Southern characters, it concentrated on the evils of slavery. Even though the story's chief villain, Simon Legree, was a transplanted Yankee in Louisiana, readers in the free states imagined Legree to be the typical Southern slaveholder. The evolving and more popular stage versions increasingly demonized Southerners. Historian Allan Nevins wrote, "The Bostonian or Clevelander seldom saw any but the highly exceptional Negro, and many people thought of them all as Frederick Douglasses. . . The South had men as . . . brutal as Legree; all societies have them. But there was no real Southern gentleman in the book." Historian Ludwell Johnson wrote, "In Legree . . . [Northerners] had what every people must have before they can fight a war with gusto, a [demonic] image of the enemy."[78]

Northern disobedience to the Fugitive Slave Act led Southerners to distrust Northern commitment to other aspects of the 1850 Compromise. Among them was the territorial option principle presumed to apply to the Utah and New Mexico Territories. As noted, Southerners objected to it in Federal territories because they felt the Constitution gave them the right to take their property, including slaves, into any territory. As Cass's local option concept evolved to become known as popular sovereignty, however, Southerners bisected it.

Significantly, Southerners concluded that popular sovereignty was illegal during a region's territorial era but acceptable when each territory petitioned for statehood. Given their presumed constitutional rights to take slaves into Federal territories, Southerners realized that popular sovereignty might provide a way to add slave states north of the 1820 Missouri Compromise line which would otherwise be impermissible. Since the geography above that latitude was generally unsuitable for slave-based agriculture, the prospects for a new slave state were slim, but better than none. Southerners were, therefore, anxious to test whether their version of popular sovereignty might yield a new slave state.

Since neither Utah nor New Mexico had enough population to apply for statehood in 1854, Southerners thought the better test would be in the lands then known as the Kansas and Nebraska territories. In addition to Kansas and Nebraska, those territories included the acreage in the Dakotas and eastern Colorado. Although

---

[78] Karen R. Smith, "Resurrection, Uncle Tom's Cabin and the Reader Crisis," *Comparative Literature Studies*, v. 33, n. 44, 1996, 350; Allan Nevins, *Ordeal of the Union: Fruits of Manifest Destiny 1847-1852* (New York: Charles Scribner's & Sons, 1947), 405-11; Harriet Beecher Stowe, *Life of Harriet Beecher Stowe*, ed. Charles Stowe (London: S. Low, Martson, Searle & Rivington, 1889) 396-97; Henry Ward Beecher, *Patriotic Addresses*, (New York: Fords, Howard & Hulbert, 1891), 167; Ludwell Johnson, *Division and Reunion*, 25.

those territories had been excluded from the 1850 Compromise, Illinois Senator Stephen Douglas wanted the Kansas and Nebraska Territories freely open to settlement so that he could promote a transcontinental railroad with an eastern terminus in Chicago to cross them. As a result, he sponsored the 1854 Kansas-Nebraska Bill, which proposed the implied popular sovereignty rights given to New Mexico and Utah be extended to Kansas and Nebraska for two reasons. First, the rights were democratic. Second, they offered the quickest way to open a Transcontinental Railroad by removing the so-called Indian barrier. President Franklin Pierce signed the bill into law in May 1854.

Abolitionists argued that the Act was an unauthorized repeal of the 1820 Missouri Compromise, even though the Kansas-Nebraska domains were unlikely to ever support slavery. But if popular sovereignty was to decide whether Kansas was to be a slave or free state, leading abolitionists resolved to populate the territory with free-state settlers. As a result, New Englanders formed the Emigrant Aid Society in April 1854 to provide financial aid to anti-slavery pioneers.

During 1854-55 the Society sent over 1,200 colonists to Kansas. But the interference annoyed so-called border ruffians from the neighboring slave state of Missouri, which hoped to migrate slave-holding families into Kansas. Consequently, several thousand Missourians crossed the border and voted illegally when Kansas elections were held in 1855. Anti-slave Kansans responded with equally illegal elections resulting in the spectacle of two rival legislatures and governments in 1856. Henry Ward Beecher sent crates of Sharps Breech-loading carbines to Society families. Shippers glibly told cooperating railroads that the heavy crates contained Beecher's Bibles. The witches brew of frauds, absentee agitation, and political exploitation caused sporadic violence culminating in May 1856 with the massacre of five men by fanatic John Brown and his sons at Pottawatomie Creek. Although the victims were pro-slavery men, none were slaveholders.

The same month the Kansas-Nebraska bill was enacted, Massachusetts Senator Charles Sumner inflamed passions with his Crime Against Kansas speech delivered at his chamber desk. Beyond exaggerating pro-slavery Kansas violence, he verbally attacked Southern politicians including South Carolina Senator Andrew Butler. Several days later a distant Butler relative, Congressman Preston Brooks, physically attacked Sumner while the latter was seated at his Senate desk. Sumner took a long convalescence as a means of exaggerating the beating for political advantage. Political leaders on both sides became irrational. Violent Kansas deaths during the six years from 1854 to 1860 only totaled about fifty, not much different than comparably populated western territories. As late as 1860 Kansas contained only two slaves.

Six months after President Pierce signed the bill, Abraham Lincoln disclosed why even non-abolitionist Proto-Republicans objected to the Act in his October 16, 1854 Peoria speech: "We want them [Federal territories] for the homes of free white people." Isolating slavery in the South would steadily reduce the South's political power whereas abolition would initially increase it by negating the three-fifths constitutional clause that limited the region's electoral college votes and House representation. Moreover, geographically confining slavery would also enable Northerners to prevent black migration into their own states or territories.

After the Kansas-Nebraska Act, more Northern states took action to protect runaway slaves by rendering the Fugitive Slave Act inoperative within their borders. Among them were Wisconsin, Ohio and Michigan. Wisconsin took a page from South Carolina's 1832-33 Nullification Act when the Badger State tried to nullify the Fugitive Slave Act with a state court ruling. In 1854 abolitionist Sherman Booth led an effort to free a slave from a Milwaukee jail with a *habeas corpus* writ. The slaveowner challenged the writ but the Wisconsin Supreme Court ruled it to be legal. The plaintiff appealed to the United States Supreme Court where the Wisconsin decision was overturned unanimously in 1859. Predictably the Washington Court cited the Constitution's Supremacy Clause, which gave the Federal courts jurisdiction because the Fugitive Slave Act was a Federal law.[79]

Although disagreements over slavery expansion became the chief focus of North-South sectional differences after the Texas annexation, it should be underscored that the North continued to use slavery as a decoy to disguise their self-serving economic ambitions—aims often detrimental to the South's economic goals. First, as explained in chapter one, as the World's low-cost producer of cotton the South's export economy thrived under the freest trade possible. From 1850 to 1859 cotton exports ranged from 48% to 59% of total American product exports annually. Other Southern exports included tobacco and the cotton feedstock sold to New England mills that constituted the raw material of exported cotton finished goods.[80]

In order to protect her economic interests, the South needed to expand the cotton domain. Failing to do so, she would not have the Senate votes needed to block future tariffs injurious to her economy. As a matter of economic survival Southerners felt compelled to seek new lands in the Southwest or elsewhere. Even though New Mexico, Kansas and Utah were unlikely prospects, they were at least hopeful ones. Without them, the planters would have to consider the West Indies and Mexico, which might require an even more difficult two-thirds vote approval in the Senate if such annexations involved international treaties.

---

[79] J. G. Randall and David Donald, *The Civil War and Reconstruction*, 94-102, 122-23; James McPherson, *Battle Cry of Freedom*, 120; Abraham Lincoln, *Peoria Speech*, (October 16, 1854) Available: https://tinyurl.com/yd2944bs [Accessed: June 9, 2020]; [79] Ludwell Johnson, *Division and Reunion*, 33-34

[80] U. S. Department of Commerce, "Historical Statistics of the United States: 1789-1945" (Washington: U. S. Government Printing Office, 1949), 247; "Growth of the Cotton Industry in America": https://www.sailsinc.org/durfee/earl2.pdf

While modern historians have condemned the South's international aspirations as empire building, it should be noted that prominent Northerners were also swept-up in the ambitions of Manifest Destiny, which one historian describes as "the belief that God was behind the American nation and that Americans were [destined] to rule over North America." Henry Raymond, who was the publisher of the *New York Times* and would later become the national chairman of the Republican Party, wrote William Yancey of Alabama about the secession crisis in December 1860:

> [If the South secedes the remaining truncated Union would] "be surrendering to a foreign and hostile power more than half of the Atlantic seaboard—the whole Gulf—the mouth of the Mississippi . . . and its drainage of the commerce from the mighty West . . . all chance of further accessions from Mexico, Central America or the West India islands and all prospect of extending our growth . . . in the only direction in which such extension will ever be possible. . .

> There is no nation in the world so ambitious for growth and power—so thoroughly pervaded with the spirit of conquest and so filled with dreams of enlarged dominions, as ours."[81]

As noted, the slave states never held a majority in the House of Representatives, and they were permanently losing any chance at parity in the Senate during the 1850s. By the end of the decade they already had a six-vote deficit in the Senate and a fifty-one-vote disadvantage in the House. When South Carolina became the first state to secede, the six vote Senate deficit was poised to become ten-votes with the admissions of Kansas and Nevada as free states. The 62%-to-38% free state advantage in the House in 1860 implied that the South would never again have the strength in the electoral

---

[81] Kenneth M. Stampp, *The Causes of the Civil War*, (New York: Touchstone, 1991), 76; Charles Adams, *When in the Course of Human Events*, 122

college to win a presidential election. In short, contrary to current propaganda, the antebellum South never controlled the Federal government. There was no mythical slavocracy ruling antebellum America.

CHAPTER 7: SLAVE POWER CONSPIRACY

IN HIS STUDY OF MASS movements Eric Hoffer explained, "Hatred is the most accessible and comprehensive of all the unifying agents. Mass movements can rise and spread without belief in a God but never without belief in a devil."

During the 1850s America's economy was doing well. Gross Domestic Product increased from $2.6 billion in 1850 to $4.4 billion in 1860 equating to a 5.5% compounded annual rate. Not only did the 1846 Walker Tariff fail to shrink the economy—as low tariff opponents argued it would—but it accelerated the expansion. Over the same period America's international trade increased from $325 million in 1850 to $700 million in 1860 yielding an 8% compounded annual growth rate. Notwithstanding the lower Walker tariffs, exports grew at a 9% yearly rate as compared to only 7% for imports. Given America's economic prosperity, the South's political enemies desired to attack her with a new weapon that avoided economic statistics. Ideally, they wanted one that could arouse moral outrage since opponents cannot easily refute an emotional narrative with facts and logic, at least in the public mind. As a result, Republicans contrived a Slave Power Conspiracy, which alleged that the South was trying to convert every state in America into a slave state.[82]

---

[82]Douglass C. North, *The United States Balance of Payments*, (Princeton: Princeton University Press, 1960), 605 Available: http://www.nber.org/chapters/c2491 [Accessed: June 7, 2020]; Ludwell Johnson, *Securing the Blessings: Today the South, Tomorrow?* Available: https://tinyurl.com/y9wrd6er [Accessed: June 7, 2020]; Eric Hoffer, *The True Believer,* (New York: Harper & Row, 1951), 91

A growing belief in the conspiracy allowed the Republican Party to rise to prominence in the North and enabled her politicians to mislead the public. After Illinois Republicans picked him as their candidate to unseat Democrat Senator Stephen Douglas in 1858, Abraham Lincoln addressed the nominating convention: "A house divided against itself cannot stand. I believe this government cannot endure permanently half slave and half free. I do not expect the Union to be dissolved—I do not expect the house to fall—but I do expect it will cease to be divided. It will become all one thing or all the other." Such words fueled the Slave Power Conspiracy by implying that Southerners wanted to turn all the states into slave states.[83]

What's worse, other remarks in that same speech reveal that Lincoln deliberately promoted the conspiracy merely to gain political advantage. Historian David Donald writes, "Lincoln was setting the stage . . . to show that Douglas was part of a dangerous plot to nationalize slavery." Lincoln implied that independent actions by Presidents James Buchanan and Franklin Pierce in combination with rulings by Chief Supreme Court Justice Roger Taney and Douglas's sponsorship of the Kansas-Nebraska Act were all parts of a conspiratorial web. Continuing his case with an analogy familiar to Illinois farmers he said, "We cannot *know*" that the four conspired. "But when we see a lot of framed timbers, different portions of which we know" were put in place by four different workmen (Pierce, Buchanan, Douglas and Taney) "and we see those timbers joined together . . . to make the frame of a house" it's obvious that the four carpenters worked from a common blueprint. One night "we shall lie down pleasantly dreaming that the people of Missouri are on the verge of making their State free

---

[83] Abraham Lincoln, "House Divided Speech," (June 16, 1858) Available: https://tinyurl.com/aq95z4v [Accessed: May 31, 2020]; David Donald, *Lincoln*, 207

and we shall awake to the reality, instead, that the Supreme Court has made Illinois a slave State."

In truth, the four men that Lincoln accused of colluding were generally not in touch. Two were even feuding. Although Douglas and Pierce cooperated to pass the 1854 Kansas-Nebraska Act, Buchanan was out of the country in diplomatic service and Taney was not involved. Additionally, Taney's 1857 Dred Scott ruling that outlawed any attempts to keep slaves out of U.S. territories was contrary to Douglas's 1858 Freeport Doctrine, which held that territorial legislatures were allowed to pass laws inhospitable to slavery. Lincoln also knew that Douglas and Buchanan were quarrelling that year over the legitimacy of Kansas's pro-slavery (Lecompton) statehood constitution. Douglas felt that the constitution was a fraud due to bogus votes by Missourians who crossed the border whereas Buchanan accepted it believing that the votes for Kansas's free state constitution were also fake. Both were correct.

Finally, Lincoln even admitted that he did not believe the tale he was spinning. When editor John Scrips told the candidate that his remarks were "an implied pledge on behalf of the Republican Party to make war upon the institution [slavery] in the states where it now exists," Lincoln walked-back his remarks. He told Scrips "that whether the clause used by me will bear such construction or not, I never so intended it." But looking for some wiggle room, Lincoln added, "I did not say I was in favor of anything . . . I made a prediction only—it may have been a foolish one perhaps." Nonetheless, he never completely disavowed his Slave Power Conspiracy fiction because it was politically useful. He realized it was convincing the Northern public that his opponents were evil fanatics set upon dominating America and putting slaves in competition with white workers in the Northern states.[84]

---

[84] David Donald, *Lincoln*, 206-09

During his famous 1858 campaign debates against Lincoln, Stephen Douglas was dismayed at Lincoln's charges that Douglas was part of such a conspiracy. In response Douglas said that he: "did not suppose there was a man in America with a heart so corrupt as to believe that such a charge could be true." After the 1857 Dred Scott case ruled that slaves could not be barred from Federal territories, Lincoln suggested the Court might soon also rule that slavery could not be barred in any state. That, he implied, would be the next step in the alleged conspiracy. Lincoln persisted in such arguments because he knew the voters would require Douglas to prove his innocence rather than demand that Lincoln prove the allegation. Opponents of Southern economic prosperity also used the technique to convince Northerners that Southerners should be required to prove that they did not intend to nationalize slavery. Southern congressmen should likewise be required to prove that their legislative proposals were free of sinister underlying motives to promote national slavery. The Conspiracy arguments caused a false Northern paranoia.

The beginnings of the Conspiracy date to Texas's 1845 annexation. From the New England Whig's perspective, the great sin was not annexation *per se*, but was two-fold. First, the joint congressional resolution authorizing annexation permitted Texas to be subdivided into as many as five separate states. Thus, Texans might unilaterally add as many as ten new Democrats to the Senate instead of only two. Northern Whigs worried that the new senators would oppose protective tariffs, public works spending, and Federal subsidies to selected businesses like New England's fishermen. Such were, after all, components of the Democrat Party line. The second factor was more immediate. Specifically, both 1846 Texas senators cast the deciding votes for the Walker Tariff that cut the rates of the 1842 Black Tariff. When Midwesterners joined Southerners to pass the Walker Bill, New Englanders fretted that the Midwesterners' need to export her growing excess grain would cause them to forge a new alliance with the South thereby strengthening congressional resistance to deterrence tariffs.

By the late 1840s slavery had come to symbolize all the underlying disputes between the North and South. But it was a mask. Historian Ludwell Johnson concluded: "Slavery, in short, was not only an issue in itself, it had also become a symbol of all the differences between the sections; that is why it became such a powerful political force. Many Northerners saw it as a moral question . . . By their nature moral questions are not subject to compromise. Therefore, it became ever more difficult for

Senator Stephen A. Douglas

the political process to get past that issue and deal with important economic and political matters that were normally amenable to negotiation, and the settlement of which would substantially have reduced the importance of the slavery controversy. The essence of the Union from its foundation had been compromise; without compromise the Union was in danger."[85]

Even though Whig candidate Zachary Taylor won the 1848 presidential election, that year also marked the emergence of the Free-Soil Party. The new Party was dedicated to reserving all Federal territories for white men, Federal funding for public works, free Federal land for western settlers, and high protective tariffs. It differed from Whig principles by its emphasis on western expansion

---

[85] Ludwell Johnson, *Division and Reunion*, 11-12

and its total ban on slaves in the Federal territories. Although some Whigs also opposed slavery expansion, many connected with the cotton textile business were prone to compromise. In taking 10% of the 1848 popular vote Free-Soilers threw New York into Taylor's win column, making him President.

Once Taylor took office the Slave Power Conspiracy was a mere fantasy by comparison to the true back-stair manipulation of the President by New York's Whig Senator William Seward. Under Seward's influence, Taylor wanted California admitted as a free state without first becoming a territory whereby slavery might be introduced into the region. Seward also persuaded Taylor that he should not veto the Wilmot Proviso should Congress renew it during his term. Seward opposed the 1850 Compromise, arguing that he was duty bound to a "higher law" than the Constitution to reject a compromise with slavery. Thus, to prevent America from becoming "all slave" Seward's position changed during the 1850s. Instead of merely wanting to quarantine it in the South, he eventually favored total abolition until he became Secretary of State in 1861.[86]

As explained in the last chapter, Northern defiance of the Fugitive Slave Act combined with California's free state admission gave the free states a numerical advantage in the Senate and left Southerners worried that the North would try to rule tyrannically with a Senate base no larger than a simple majority. Although the territories west of the Missouri River offered anti-slavery elements abundant lands where they might colonize new states, Southern slavery could not sensibly expand into the desert lands west of Texas. Nonetheless, Northerners interpreted any attempt to provide new lands for Southern expansion as evidence of an omnipotent Slave Power Conspiracy. In addition to the Kansas-

---

[86] William H. Seward, "Irrepressible Conflict Speech," (October 25, 1858), Available: https://tinyurl.com/6mn64o5, [Accessed: June 1, 2020]; David Potter, *The Impending Crisis*, 96

Nebraska Act, Northerners reacted with frenzy to an unapproved diplomatic initiative that might have added a new slave state. Known as the Ostend Manifesto, it happened while Franklin Pierce was President.

After Pierce took office in 1853, he wanted to expand America's borders. Therefore, in April 1854 Secretary of State William Marcy told America's ambassador to Spain that he should offer $130 million for Cuba. If Spain declined the offer, Ambassador Pierre Soulé was instructed to "detach" the island from Spain. When Spain rejected Soulé's proposal, he asked that the American ministers to France and Great Britain meet with him to discuss the situation. As a result, James Buchanan, John Mason and Soulé met at Ostend, Belgium. The three prepared a paper that became known as the Ostend Manifesto and sent it to Pierce. It urged that Cuba be taken by force if the island was judged to be a military threat to the United States. Even though Pierce overruled the advice, Northern cynics construed the affair to be a sinister example of the Slave Power Conspiracy's attempt to add a new slave state.

Such charges were not only fanciful, but also hypocritical. Many Northerners held fast to their own dreams of Manifest Destiny with nearly insatiable desires to expand America's frontiers. While serving as Secretary of State under Andrew Johnson, William Seward negotiated with Russia to buy Alaska in 1867. After he became President in 1869 Ulysses Grant tried to annex the island of Santo Domingo, which includes the present nations of Haiti and the Dominican Republic. Veterans marching in support of his campaign "made exuberant declarations that the Stars and Stripes should fly over Canada and Mexico." Massachusetts Senator Charles Sumner, Chair the Foreign Affairs Committee from 1861 to 1871, hoped for years to annex Canada as did Bay State Congressman and Civil War Major General Benjamin Butler.[87]

---

[87] David Potter, *The Impending Crisis*, 349-50; William Hesseltine, *Ulysses Grant*

Earlier examples of Northern territorial ambitions date to the War of 1812. American armies from the Northeast and Midwest attempted to annex Canada but their invasions were turned back. In 1846 the joint British-American occupation of the Oregon Country ended by granting America everything below the forty-ninth parallel. Despite arguing against slavery and its Southern expansion, in 1850 Seward remarked on his low opinion of blacks and his own chauvinistic territorial aspirations. During a Senate speech favoring California statehood he said, "[America] consists of natives of Caucasian origin and exotics of the same derivation. The native mass rapidly assimilates itself and absorbs the exotics. The African race . . . and the aborigines . . . constitute inferior masses [that cannot assimilate.] . . . The Atlantic states . . . are steadily renovating . . . Europe and Africa. The Pacific states must necessarily perform the same . . . beneficent functions in Asia. . . [to create] a new and more perfect civilization . . . under the sway of our own cherished and beneficent democratic institutions."[88]

After the United States acquired California and settled Oregon's boundary in the 1840s, motivated leaders began to dream of the wealth that might be won by tapping the fabled markets of the Far East. While the country's new deep-water ports on the Pacific Coast could serve the trans-Pacific link, her intended transcontinental railroad could carry cargoes to the Atlantic and thence to Europe. Future acquisition of Mexico and Central America might enable a cross-isthmus canal controlled by the United States. In short, ambitious Americans envisioned that the United States might become a vast commercial highway connecting Europe with the Far East. Northerners held such ambitions at least as firmly as

Politician, (New York: Dodd & Mead, 1935) 196, 223; Chester G. Hearn, *Gray Raiders of the Sea,* (Camden, Me.: International Marine Publishing, 1992), 304

[88] William H. Seward, *The Works of William H. Seward: Vol. 1* (New York: Redfield, 1853), 56, 58; Morison and Commager *The Growth of the American Republic: Volume 1,* 410, 418-19

Southerners. Moreover, they were fully aware that such aspiring dreams would require annexation of territories where slavery might prosper. When obsessed with a vision of a Pax Americana to rival the ancient Pax Romana, men with such dreams gave little thought to slavery.[89]

Four months after Lincoln's June 1858 House Divided Speech, William Seward added his voice to the Slave Conspiracy theory in an address he delivered as the then-leading Republican contender for the 1860 Party's nomination: "Shall I tell you what this collision [between slave and free states] means? It is an irrepressible conflict between opposing and enduring forces, and it means that the United States must and will, sooner or later, become either entirely a slaveholding nation, or entirely a free-labor nation. Either the cotton and rice fields of South Carolina . . . will ultimately be tilled by free [non-slave] labor . . . or else the rye fields and wheat fields of Massachusetts and New York must again be surrendered . . . to the production of slaves."

After 1856 the Free-Soil Party evolved into the Republican Party, which had minimal appeal south of the Ohio River and Mason Dixon Line. Its leaders, such as Lincoln and Seward, continued to frighten free state voters with reckless Slave Power speculations. They argued that the Dred Scott ruling, which applied to Federal *territories*, might be extended in a hypothetical future case to apply to all the *states*. In the unlikely event of such a case, and ruling, the free states could seek to amend the Constitution. They probably could have won ratification for the simple reason that Southerners did not want to transplant slavery into a region where residents had demonstrated decades earlier that it was impractical. Almost three years after the actual Dred Scott ruling, the 1860 census revealed

---

[89] Ludwell Johnson, *Division and Reunion*, 30-31

that only 46 slaves and 20 slave owners lived in all the Federal territories west of the Mississippi River.

Instead of constituting a potent force to nationalize slavery, the South's political power had been shrinking for years. Between 1845 and the start of the Civil War in 1861 no slave states joined the Union, whereas six free states were added. Additionally, by totaling only one percent of America's population in 1860 the number of slaveholders was too small to compose a dominant class.

The South was undeniably falling behind in terms of population growth. Of America's 8.5 million population gain in the 1850s, the Southern states accounted for only 2 million. In contrast the Midwest, from the Ohio River to Dakota Territory, gained 3.7 million. Even as the population of the older Northern states of New York and Pennsylvania gained 1.5 million people, the older Southern states of Virginia, North Carolina and South Carolina increased their combined population by less than 0.3 million. Especially significant was the shift in Midwestern trade from the South to the Northeast via the Great Lakes and trunk line railroads as opposed to the Mississippi River. In 1850 the region sent 40% of its corn down the Mississippi and 60% to the Northeast. By 1860 it sent only 20% down the Mississippi and 80% to the Northeast. In 1850 it sent 80% of its pork to the South but less than 40% by 1860. In 1850 the Midwest sent 9% of its wheat South but only 2% in 1860.

In truth, the Slave Power Conspiracy was a delusion that provided paranoid Northerners with an all-encompassing explanation for whatever seemed threatening. When dominated by such misconceptions, Hoffer's "true believers" ignore facts contrary to their beliefs.[90]

---

[90] Ludwell Johnson, "Securing the Blessing: Today the South, Tomorrow ?" Available: https://tinyurl.com/y9wrd6er [Accessed: June 3, 2020]; Allan Nevins, *The Emergence of Lincoln: 1859-1861* (New York: Charles Scribner, 1950), 309-311

Meanwhile, Stephen Douglas's popular sovereignty was proving to be a practical method for isolating slavery in the fifteen slave states admitted prior to 1846. Despite its effectiveness in blocking slavery expansion, by 1855 Southerners accepted popular sovereignty as a legitimate way for territories to petition for statehood. At that juncture, Southerners recognized a popular vote to be a legitimate way to determine whether the applicable state should be admitted as either slave or free. They objected to its use during the territorial stage because it would provide a disincentive for taking slaves into the territories thereby making all future states free states by default.

During the 1860 presidential election both Douglas, of the Northern Democrat Party, and John C. Breckinridge, of the Southern Democrat Party, favored popular sovereignty at the time of statehood. They differed over Douglas's Freeport Doctrine which permitted the people, or legislatures, of each territory to pass laws inhospitable to slavery even before the territory petitioned for statehood. The Doctrine informed slaveholders that even though they had a constitutional right to take their slaves into Federal territories, they could not enforce that right if the applicable territory wanted to exclude slavery.[91]

The supreme effort to expand slavery into a geographically dubious region failed in Kansas. If the so-called slaveocracy could not succeed in Kansas, it could not succeed in any of the remaining Federal territories. The Nebraska Territory, which included the Dakotas, was safely distant from slavery because her settlers would come from the adjacent free states of Iowa and Minnesota, as well as points east. Nevada was in California's orbit and Colorado was even less suited for slavery than Kansas. The only hope for

---

[91] David Potter, *The Impending Crisis,* 338, Digital History, *Democratic Platform, 1860 (Breckinridge faction),* Available: https://tinyurl.com/y8mcxcax [Accessed: June 28, 2020]

slaveholders was that future Federal territories might be acquired farther south, such as in the Caribbean.

Kansas was a natural destination for emigrants from Missouri, a slave state. When Kansas elected its first territorial legislature in March 1855 some Missourians crossed the border to stuff the ballot boxes for pro-slavery candidates. The resulting legislature met at Shawnee Mission and drafted a code that limited future legislators to pro-slavery men. Opposing Kansans responded by repudiating the Shawnee Mission government. They met in Topeka and drafted a free-state constitution, which they submitted for voter approval. The Topeka constitution outlawed the immigration of slaves and free blacks. Although a popular vote ratified the Topeka constitution, pro-slavery residents boycotted that election because they had already accepted the Shawnee Mission government. As a result, 1856 Kansas had two irregular and rival governments. Washington had to settle on one.

Lincoln-Douglas Debates 1858

That summer Georgia Senator Robert Toombs offered a three-step plan to resolve the question. First would be a special presidential census to verify and complete Kansas's voter rolls.

Second, the census-verified voters would choose delegates for a state constitutional convention. Third, convention delegates would write a constitution and submit it to the voters for ratification. Toombs's goal was to insure a fair vote. Nonetheless, Republicans objected by claiming that they did not believe a Pierce appointee would conduct a fair census. Thus, the Kansas problem rolled over to the Buchanan Administration, which assumed office in March 1857. Buchanan took the position that the Kansas-Nebraska Act required that the slave-or-free status of Kansas statehood be determined by popular sovereignty. He ordered a census in the spring of 1857

Unfortunately, many of the free-state settlers drove off, or evaded, census takers because they wanted to avoid having their names added to the tax rolls. Since only taxpayers could vote in the delegate election, pro-slavery delegates dominated the convention that met at Lecompton. They drew up two nearly identical constitutions with only a single difference. The pro-slavery version would allow slaveholders to immigrate to the state with their slaves thereby making Kansas a slave state. The alternate version prohibited any new slaves but allowed the owners of the small number of slaves already in the territory to keep them.

Meanwhile Kansas held an October election for territorial legislators that allowed non-taxpaying residents to vote. Initial returns yielded a pro-slavery legislative majority, but the temporary governor threw out the tallies of two counties where Missourian's had voted fraudulently. Even though he lacked authority to discard the returns, a free-state-majority territorial legislature convened on 7 December and passed a law blocking any referendum that only gave voters a choice between one of two constitutions. As a result, free-state voters boycotted the December 21, 1857 referendum that ratified the pro-slavery Lecompton constitution. Next, the free-state legislature scheduled their own referendum for January 1858 that would allow voters to reject both Lecompton constitutions and hold a simultaneous election to choose new officeholders. Since pro-slavery voters abstained during the January vote, both versions of the Lecompton constitutions were rejected by free-state supporters and they also again put Republicans in charge of nearly all political offices.

Since the two sides boycotted the elections of the opposing side, President Buchanan was forced to make a choice. He chose to support the pro-slavery Lecompton constitution arguing that if Kansans were really opposed to slavery as the free state voters claimed, they could change the constitution after the state was admitted to the Union. Opponents argued that certain terms of the constitution made it impossible to execute changes quickly. For example, no amendments would be allowed until 1864. Finally, Congress agreed to let Kansans have one final vote on the pro-slavery Lecompton constitution. If they accepted it, Kansas would immediately become a slave state. If they rejected it, Kansas would not be allowed to apply for statehood until she met the normal population threshold required for statehood. Kansans rejected the Lecompton constitution by a vote of about 11,000-to-2,000 in August 1858. Popular sovereignty had stopped the expansion of slavery.[92]

Once popular sovereignty demonstrated that it could restrict slavery to the South, Republicans had only one reason to deny slaveholders the right to take slaves into the Federal territories: *to save their own Party.* The decisive 1858 free state victory enabled by popular sovereignty in Kansas showed that Republicans had needlessly inflamed sectional animosity by demanding a blanket

---

[92] David Potter, *The Impending Crisis*, 306-317; Ludwell Johnson, *Division and Reunion*, 49-52; J. G. Randall and David Donald, *The Civil War and Reconstruction*, 99-100; Allan Nevins, *The Emergence of Lincoln: 1857-59* (New York: Charles Scribner's & Sons, 1950), 234-35, 269-70

ban on slaves in the territories. Putting slavery aside, their Party's economic principles were mostly like those of the Whigs. In short, popular sovereignty obviated the need for the Republican Party.

Absent the Republican self-preservation instinct, popular sovereignty could have contained slavery in the South while America continued peacefully as a united country indefinitely. The Lincoln and Seward House Divided speeches dog-whistled to Northerners a dread for the imagined Slave Power plan to nationalize slavery. Without such a phantom devil the Republicans might have followed the Free-Soilers into oblivion. In the forthcoming 1860 presidential election, only the Republican Party opposed popular sovereignty. Every vote for Abraham Lincoln was a vote to risk Southern secession whereas a vote for Breckinridge or Douglas was a vote for popular sovereignty.

The 1858 pacification of Kansas relaxed sectional tensions even in the South where the economy was strong. The national GDP grew at a 2.5% annual rate over the next thirty months notwithstanding the 1857 Ohio Insurance Company financial panic. The 1858 cotton crop was the second largest in history and prices were high. Scientific farming techniques were improving the productivity in even the oldest Southern states such as South Carolina. Although small, the region's value of manufacturing had doubled during the 1850s. At the end of the decade railroads had connected the South Atlantic with the Mississippi River. The region's healthy economy offset Southern worries over the future of slavery. It's unlikely that a single state could have been persuaded to leave the Union unless conditions changed.

But conditions changed when John Brown tried to start a slave insurrection at Harpers Ferry in October 1859. Although not a single slave joined the grandiose scheme, it pushed Southern anxieties into high gear. Since there had not been a major slave uprising in nearly thirty years the incident might have been dismissed as the lone act of a lunatic until investigators made three discoveries. First, Brown hoped to extend the uprising across the entire South. He had even written a constitution for a new country he planned to carve out of the region. Second, Brown would not hesitate to kill resisting slaveowners and authorized his followers to confiscate the owners' non-slave property. Third, investigators discovered that six prominent New Englanders had financially backed the scheme, while other abolitionists such as Frederick Douglass were aware of it but kept quiet.

Four months after his 1856 Kansas murders at Pottawattamie Creek, Brown moved East. He first stopped in Cincinnati to get a character reference from Republican leader Salmon P. Chase. He was already carrying one from Kansas Republican Charles Robinson. Upon arriving in Massachusetts, literary legends Ralph Waldo Emerson and Henry David Thoreau warmly welcomed him and provided introductions to other intellectuals. Eventually their network opened the doors to the secret six.

Emerson protégé Franklin Sanborn was the youngest. A second was Dr. Samuel Howe, a leading abolitionist whose wife would later compose the lyrics for the *Battle Hymn of the Republic*. George L. Stearns was another. He became so fascinated by Brown that he compared him to George Washington. A fourth was the multilingual Theodore Parker who had authored one of the most informed books on slavery. Gerrit Smith was the fifth. He inherited his wealth from his father who was a partner with John Jacob Astor in the fur trading days. Last was Thomas Wentworth Higginson who said he was "always ready to invest in treason." During the Civil War he joined the Union army and commanded a regiment of black troops.

Brown met with the six men several times in 1858-59. All generally knew what he planned but asked not to be too well informed so that they may deflect questions later if the conspiracy failed and they became exposed. None could doubt that Brown was prepared to massacre Southern whites who might resist his followers, yet the six were indifferent to such consequences.

Even after the secret backers were disclosed, New England intellectuals praised Brown. In his *Plea for Captain John Brown*

Thoreau proclaimed him "an angel of light." Parker said that Brown was a saint whose slave rebellion could only be "extinguished with white man's blood." *Little Women* author, Louisa May Alcott bestowed upon him the title, "St. John the Just." To Ralph Waldo Emerson, Brown was also a holy person "whose martyrdom . . . would make the gallows as sacred as the cross."[93]

During his incarceration and trial other Northerners increasingly sympathized with Brown. Soon-to-be-Massachusetts-Governor John Andrew said, "I only know that whether the enterprise itself was one or the other [right or wrong], but John Brown himself was right." Even the politically cagey William Seward wrote his wife that Brown was "morally above his prosecutors so much that you almost forget his criminality." After he was hanged on December 2, 1859 abolitionists Joshua Giddings wrote that "the hatred of slavery [was] greatly intensified by the fate of Brown and his men . . . [thereby making other] . . . men . . . ready to march on Virginia and dispose of her despotism at once." Historian Allan Nevins wrote, "Most Northerners believed that the man's [Brown's] character was noble, that his errors were those of a fanatic, and that if his act condemned himself, it also condemned slavery. It is the heaviest blow yet struck against the institution, said some, it brings the end of slavery ten years nearer, said others." All across the North men gathered to mourn Brown's passing and express their anger at the South. Consequently, more Southerners than ever were ready to consider secession.[94]

---

[93] Ludwell Johnson, *Division and Reunion*, 58-59
[94] *Ibid.*: 60; Allan Nevins, *The Emergence of Lincoln: 1859-61*, 99

CHAPTER 8: COMPROMISE ATTEMPTS

THE DEMOCRAT PARTY'S presidential nominating convention opened on April 23, 1860 in Charleston, South Carolina. Republicans began theirs about three weeks later in Chicago on 16 May. The Democrats correctly presumed that the Republican platform would require that slaves be banned from all Federal territories. Consequently, the chief debate in Charleston was over how to respond to the anticipated Republican plank. The larger faction led by Stephen A. Douglas would leave the status of territorial slaves for the Supreme Court, which ruled in the 1857 Dred Scott decision that they could not be barred. As noted in the preceding chapter, Douglas's platform would also permit the territories to achieve statehood as either free or slave based upon a popular vote by the people in the applicable territory under the doctrine of popular sovereignty. A smaller faction led by Alabama's William Yancey demanded that the Republican ban on territorial slaves be countered by a Democrat plank that guaranteed slaveowners access to all Federal territories before each territory voted on statehood. Yancey did not want to rely only upon a Supreme Court ruling. His was mostly a stand on constitutional principle, instead of practicality, because none of the remaining Federal territories in 1860 were suitable for slavery.

Since the differences could not be reconciled, the Charleston convention collapsed on 3 May when Yancey's delegates walked out. It reconvened in Baltimore on 16 June without the Yancey faction and nominated Douglas for President. The Southern delegates met separately and nominated the then-current Vice President, John C. Breckinridge, as their candidate. Breckinridge's platform answered the Republican territorial slave policy with two planks. One required that all citizens, including slaveholders, have unrestricted access to the Federal territories. A second stipulated that popular sovereignty be applied when territories petitioned for statehood, as did Douglas's.[95]

When the Democrat Party split two weeks before the Republicans convened in Chicago the latter sensed victory in the general election even if they only won electoral votes from free states. In 1856 the Democrats won four Northern states; Pennsylvania, New Jersey, Illinois and Indiana. Republicans only needed to win Pennsylvania and one of the other four to clinch victory. As a result, they tried to pick a candidate that could best carry the needed states, which proved to be Abraham Lincoln. Although New York's William Seward was better known, he had been a Party leader for over ten years and accumulated intra-party enemies. Lincoln also benefitted from a long association with Henry Clay's American System favoring protective tariffs. Lincoln's campaign operatives met with Pennsylvania's Simon Cameron, who headed the state's delegation, to assure him of their candidate's appreciation for protective tariffs, which were crucial to the Keystone State's iron industry. Finally, Lincoln's convention managers indicated that Cameron and Indiana's Caleb Smith could expect cabinet posts should Lincoln become President. Lincoln won the nomination on the third ballot. [96]

A fourth contender, Tennessee's John Bell, entered the contest under the Constitutional Union Party, which emphasized traditional interpretations of the Constitution and Union. It was silent on slavery and appealed mostly to the border states where Lincoln's support was negligible, and Douglas and Breckinridge were thought to be too factional. All four candidates disavowed

[95] Digital History, "Democratic Platform, 1860 (Douglas faction)" Available: https://tinyurl.com/r7c3a5m [Accessed: June 12, 2020]; Digital History, "Democratic Platform, 1860 (Breckinridge faction)" Available: https://tinyurl.com/y8mcxcax [Accessed: June 12, 2020]; J. G. Randall and David Donald, *The Civil War and Reconstruction*, 132; Ludwell Johnson, *Division and Reunion*, 65
[96] Ludwell Johnson, *Division and Reunion*, 62-64

secession. Yet, according to historian Ludwell Johnson "in the deep South there was a powerful minority willing to accept secession and perhaps an even larger element among the Republicans willing to put down secession by force."[97]

Douglas personally campaigned the hardest. Lincoln left the job to professional agents who organized boisterous marches and demonstrations financed by the Party loyal with a full campaign chest. Among the marchers were a multi-state group of Wide Awakes, which was a belligerent paramilitary youth organization taught to hate Southerners through fables about the Slave Power Conspiracy. Lincoln was kept off the ballot in Southern states with a total of sixty-one electoral votes while Breckinridge was off the ballot in Northern states containing seventy-three votes.

All Parties minimized slavery and pretended that secession was not an issue. Even though Southerners were well aware of the "all slave or all free" implications of Lincoln's House Divided speech, he made no effort to reassure them that he would not abolish slavery or fail to compensate them if he did. While Southerners knew they did not want to nationalize slavery, they waited in vain for Lincoln to clarify whether he intended to abolish it. They longed for clarification because his previous public remarks were contradictory.[98]

Due to the split in the Democrat Party, Lincoln won a majority of the electoral votes even though he had just 40% of the popular vote, while Douglas got 30%, Breckinridge 18% and Bell 12%. After Pennsylvania voted in October everyone knew Lincoln was President-elect by the end of that month. Two weeks later South Carolina's legislature authorized a secession convention in December. By the time Congress assembled on 3 December the legislatures of six additional Gulf States from Georgia to Texas had called for secession conventions. The nation was in shock, but the other slave states waited to see how the Federal Government would

[97] *Ibid.*; 65-66
[98] J. G. Randall and David Donald, *The Civil War and Reconstruction*, 135-36

respond. In his annual December message Buchanan stated that even though the Constitution did not authorize secession, neither did it permit him to coerce a seceded state back into the Union. Even if he had such power, he concluded that a Union held together by bayonets was worse than none at all. He suggested amendments to reassure the South that her minority rights would not be trampled if she remained in the Union.

Meanwhile the House and Senate organized committees to arrange a compromise. Owing to its higher status, the Senate Committee of Thirteen became the more important one. Kentucky Senator John Crittenden introduced the chief plan, known as the Crittenden Compromise. Its two main provisions assured better enforcement of the Fugitive Slave Act and official protection for slavery in the Federal territories South of the latitude that included Missouri's lower border, extended westward to California. Basically, it was an extension of the 1820 Missouri Compromise line. It would allow slavery in the present-day states of Arizona and New Mexico even though their lands were inhospitable to slave agriculture. Nonetheless, Committee Republicans unanimously rejected the compromise. Crittenden later tried to get it submitted to America's voters as a referendum, but most congressional Republicans voted against the motion thereby blocking a national plebiscite. They realized that the referendum would likely succeed, even among Northern voters.

If passed, such a referendum would ruin the Republican Party because it would demonstrate that a blanket ban on slaves in all Federal territories was more extreme than necessary to contain slavery. The ban served no purpose other than antagonizing sectional relations. Experts generally agree that the Party's survival instinct influenced, perhaps governed, Republican policy. Historian Kenneth Stampp concluded: "Thus, it is all too evident that reunion through compromise was impossible without the death of the Republican party, and there were few of its members who chose to make that sacrifice." Similarly, one Ohio Republican wrote

Treasury Secretary Chase, "If Fort Sumter is evacuated, the new administration is done forever, the Republican Party is done."[99]

No one realized the Party's likely extinction if it adopted popular sovereignty, or otherwise compromised, more than President-elect Lincoln. During December 1860 he wrote letter after letter to Party members urging no compromise. On 10 December he told one senator, "Let there be no compromise on the question of extending slavery. . . Have none of it. Stand firm." To William Seward's behind-the-scenes politico, Thurlow Weed, Lincoln wrote, "[be] inflexible on the territorial question." He expected Weed to pass the message along to a pending meeting of Republican governors.[100]

The biggest objection Republicans had to the Crittenden Compromise was its provision allowing slavery in the Federal territories below the latitude of Missouri's southern border. They were less concerned about the New Mexico Territory than such lands as might be acquired in the future. As written, the Crittenden Compromise would allow slavery in lands "hereafter acquired." Should Manifest Destiny turn south, Mexico, Central America and the Caribbean might provide new slave states. Paranoid Republicans imagined the provision was written expressly for that purpose and, therefore, a fresh example of the Slave Power Conspiracy.

Remarks by New York Republican Congressman Roscoe Conkling illustrate how exaggerated such fears had become. In a House address he argued that the provision "would amount to a perpetual covenant of war against every people, tribe, and State owning a foot of land between here and Terra del Fuego." In short, Conkling and other Republicans believed the latitude demarcation threatened the North's supremacy by possibly opening new lands

---

[99] Kenneth Stampp, *And the War Came*, 156-57; Maury Klein, *Days of Defiance* (New York: Vintage Books, 1999), 355

[100] Ludwell Johnson, *Division and Reunion*, 68-69; David M. Potter, *The Impending Crisis*, 534; The Crittenden Compromise is often said to have a third major component guaranteeing that the Federal government would never interfere with slavery where it was already legal. That provision, however, was redundant to the original constitution.

amenable to the South's slave economy in future American expansion.[101]

Their anxieties were unreasonable for three reasons. First, without the "hereafter acquired" clause only unsuitable expansion lands would be available to slaveholders. Second, the South was politically too weak to control the direction of America's future growth. In 1860 slave state senators were outnumbered 36-to-30 whereas Southern House members were outnumbered 149-to-88. No expansion below the pertinent latitude could take place without significant Northern agreement, particularly if the expansion involved an international treaty that would need a two-thirds approval vote in the Senate. Third, many Northerners lusted for new territories as much as Southerners.

Chicago's Methodist Bishop Matthew Simpson, for example, opined that the American flag should eventually fly "over the whole western hemisphere," and then "we must take the world in our arms and convert all other nations to our true form of government." As noted in chapter six, during the secession crisis Henry T. Raymond, who owned *The New York Times* and would later become Republican Party Chairman wrote Alabama's William Yancey: "There is no nation in the world so ambitious for growth and power—so thoroughly pervaded with the spirit of conquest and so filled with dreams of enlarged dominions, as ours. "[102]

South Carolina started the Southern secession march on December 20, 1860. Federal employees residing in the state resigned. Aside from a lingering postal service, within days the state's only Federal presence was a band of less than one hundred soldiers at Fort Moultrie in Charleston Harbor under the command of Major Robert Anderson, a West Point graduate and slaveowner from Kentucky. Since Moultrie was vulnerable to attack from its

---

[101] Kenneth Stampp, *And the War Came,* 169

[102] William H. Seward, *The Works of William H. Seward: Vol. 1,* 56, 58; Ludwell Johnson, "Securing the Blessing: Today the South, Tomorrow?" Available: https://tinyurl.com/y9wrd6er [Accessed: June 3, 2020]; Augustus Maverick, *Henry J. Raymond and the New York Press,* (Hartford, Ct.: A. S. Hale, 1870), 418

landward side, Anderson secretly moved his men to Fort Sumter on the night of 26 December. Although unfinished, Sumter was a more powerful citadel located on an island in the harbor. While Anderson and President Buchanan regarded the move as an unoffensive defensive measure, the South Carolinians interpreted it as a hostile intent by a foreign power to hold a military facility within the borders of an independent state. It was one of a growing number of examples where a single event had different interpretations depending upon the observer's political perspective. To Southerners, for example, secession was legal because it was not prohibited by the Constitution whereas Northerners regarded it as illegal because the Constitution did not authorize it.

During his time at Fort Moultrie, Major Anderson had asked Washington for reinforcements, but once safely in Fort Sumter he no longer felt a need for more troops. Since he was unable to promptly update Washington, Army Commander Lieutenant General Winfield Scott and President Buchanan organized a relief expedition.

Initially, they intended to send Anderson 250 more soldiers aboard the warship USS *Brooklyn*. Upon reflection, however, Scott recommended that the *Brooklyn* be replaced by an unarmed merchant steamer, which he thought would be less provocative. Accordingly, he leased the side-wheeler *Star of the West*, which arrived at the mouth of Charleston Harbor on the morning of January 9, 1861. Having secretly learned of the *Star's* mission, South Carolina batteries on the mainland turned her back with modest damage before she could reach Sumter. Since Anderson was unaware of the *Star's* purpose, he declined to open fire against the Carolina batteries even though he could have overwhelmed them. Although Washington had sent him orders to "silence" the Carolina batteries should they shoot at the *Star*, the message arrived too late. It is interesting to speculate what would have happened if the *Brooklyn* had been sent as originally planned instead of the *Star of the West*.

Major Robert Anderson

Since the *Brooklyn* had been under orders to deliver supplies and soldiers to Sumter, it almost certainly would have returned fire to the Carolina batteries. It had the strength to fight past them and relieve Fort Sumter. Furthermore, *Brooklyn's* gunfire would likely have prompted Sumter to retaliate as well. The meager Carolina batteries available in early January had no chance against such combined firepower. Afterward, *Brooklyn* could have sailed three miles upstream to the Charleston wharves, eliminating whatever resistance it might meet along the way. Once there, it could demand the city's surrender under its frowning guns. That's how events happened a year later when federal warships, including the *Brooklyn*, fought past two forts guarding New Orleans, the Confederacy's biggest city. If she had departed when originally scheduled, before the switch to the *Star*, the *Brooklyn* might have aborted the entire war before any other state seceded.

Although *Brooklyn's* sixteen-foot draft may have been too deep for adroit maneuvering in Charleston Harbor, a smaller warship might have been substituted. One example was the USS *Pawnee*, which was stationed near Washington during the first three months of 1861. She drew only ten feet and might have been accompanied by a second vessel to transport the reinforcing troops.[103]

Be that as it may, by February 2, 1861 the six Gulf states joined South Carolina in secession and a few days later formed the Confederate States of America (C.S.A.). Some, including South

---

[103] Philip Leigh, "Preempting the Civil War," *Lee's Lost Dispatch and Other Civil War Controversies,* (Yardley, Pa.: Westholme Publishing, 2015), 30, 32, 34-38

Carolina, Mississippi, Texas and Georgia, prepared *Declarations of Causes* for secession. Although the *Declarations* often refer to state sovereignty, unequal access to common Federal territories, grievances concerning broken agreements, and the compact nature of America's Constitution, they also defend slavery. Most modern historians focus on the last point to conclude that slavery caused secession and therefore caused of the Civil War. They minimize non-slave provisions of the Confederate Constitution notwithstanding that such provisions disclose additional secession motives. Today's historians also usually fail to question the false premise that secession must necessarily have led to war. The Confederate Constitution will be analyzed in the chapter nine and the false premise equating secession to war shall be discussed in chapter ten.

The other eight slave states also turned their attention toward secession. After Delaware's legislature permitted a roving commissioner from Mississippi to address both chambers, they adopted a resolution condemning the Magnolia State's secession. Although urged to call a special legislative session to consider secession, Maryland Governor Thomas Hicks declined. He opposed secession although a significant number of legislators from the eastern part of the state wanted to consider it.

In late January North Carolina put the matter to its voters. It simultaneously allowed them to choose delegates to a secession convention and decide whether they even wanted the convention to convene. Most of the delegates they elected opposed secession and by a narrow margin North Carolinians even voted against holding the convention. Tennessee resolved to hold a secession convention in late February. The authorization stipulated that the state's voters must validate the decision in a plebiscite should it choose secession. Kentucky's legislature considered secession in late January and recommended that a national convention be organized to develop a peaceful compromise, suggesting Senator Crittenden's.

Missouri's legislature authorized a secession convention for 18 February. On 19 March it voted 98-to-1 against secession. An Arkansas convention that initially adjourned on 21 March decided to put the matter to the voters in August, although the convention could reconvene should political circumstances change.

Virginia was the most important uncommitted slave state. She had the largest population of all slave states. As the home of Presidents Washington, Jefferson, Madison, Monroe and Tyler, she also had the strongest ties to the Federal Union and America's tradition. Although wanting to keep his state in the Union, Governor John Letcher made it clear that Virginians would not tolerate a forcible return of any cotton state to the Union. Even though he did not yet want to organize a secession convention, his legislature demanded one. They passed a resolution calling for a "Peace Conference" of states to meet in Washington on 4 February. They also authorized a secession convention for Virginia to convene on 13 February. Although conducted under the leadership of former President John Tyler, the Peace Conference accomplished little beyond echoing Crittenden's proposal. The state convention concluded that if peace between the cotton state Confederacy and the Federal Union could not be achieved, Virginia should side with the cotton states, which had recently organized the C.S.A.[104]

---

[104] Bruce Catton, *The Coming Fury*, (London: Phoenix Press, 2001), 193-97

CHAPTER 9: CONFEDERATE GOVERNMENT

THE SEVEN COTTON STATES formed a provisional Constitution for the Confederate States of America at Montgomery, Alabama. It became effective on February 8, 1861. Although modeled after the Federal Constitution it had significant differences, mostly designed to avoid a concentration of power by maximizing the rights and responsibilities of the states and limiting those of the Central Government. The first difference was in the Preamble. The Federal one begins: "We the People of the United States. . ." The Confederate Constitution adds a qualifying phrase stressing individual state sovereignty. Instead of "We the People," they wrote: "We, the people of the Confederate States, each State acting in its sovereign and independent character. . ."

During the preceding seventy-two years Confederate founders, their parents and grandparents had watched as the Federal Government became manipulated by crony capitalists who secured favors from the Central Government in order to subsidize public works and selected industries. Consequently, the Confederate Constitution outlawed such programs, with minor exceptions. It also dropped the "general welfare" clause in the Federal Constitution's spending authority, which Northerners often used as a green light for public spending programs. In contrast, the Confederate Constitution stipulated that taxes could be spent for only three purposes: military defense, government operating expenses, and the repayment of national debts.

To minimize pork-barrel projects, only the President could normally put bills before the Confederate Congress. All bills had to state the amount of money required and the title had to identify the object of the spending. The provision basically eliminated omnibus spending bills. Cost overruns were not allowed. The minority of bills that might originate in Congress would require a two-thirds majority vote of each house to be enacted. Confederate Presidents would be allowed to veto individual components of an appropriations bill whereas Federal Presidents could only veto the entire bill. The Confederate Constitution outlawed protective tariffs. No duties could be used to "promote or foster any branch of industry." Other business subsidies were also outlawed.

Regarding slavery, the Constitution stipulated that the slaveholder's rights to his property could not be restricted if he were to move, or travel, with them to any territory or state of the Confederacy. It did not prevent any member state from abolishing slavery within its own borders. Such a state could not, however, prevent slaveholders from moving into, or traveling across it. Thus, if it were an area where slavery might prosper it may well become a de-facto slave state. But if it were an area unsuitable for slavery, the institution would most likely never take root. Finally, the Constitution outlawed international slave trade and authorized Congress to outlaw it with any of the slave states remaining in the U.S.A.

Confederate founders were also concerned about bureaucratic creep, which could lead to a tyrannical Central Government in the form of a Deep-State of career administrators. Consequently, each state was empowered to impeach officials of the Central Government operating exclusively in their state. It required a two-thirds vote of both houses of the state's legislature. Such officials would be tried by the C.S.A.'s Senate, with a two-thirds vote required for conviction. Another safeguard against a too-powerful Central Government was the stipulation that constitutional amendments could only originate with the states. Although they could not be introduced in Congress, any three states could form a convention to propose new amendments. Finally, each President was limited to a single six-year term.[105]

The Confederacy never organized a Supreme Court because her founders generally interpreted the U.S. Constitution strictly. Although authorized to form one, they were never satisfied that they had developed a method that would prevent the Court from exceeding its authority. Previously they had observed that the U.S. Supreme Court tended to make rulings, and assume jurisdictions, that strengthened the Federal Government. As a component of that Government they realized the Court had an organic tendency to increase its authority. Along with some of the best-informed founders of the 1789 Federal Union, they believed that the Supreme Court was only intended to be the final authority on matters pertaining to the powers specifically enumerated in the U.S. Constitution. None of the three Federal branches—President, Congress or Judiciary—were intended to have final authority over the rights reserved for the states.

During the controversy over President Adams's 1798 Sedition Act discussed in chapter one, James Madison denied that the Supreme Court was the ultimate authority on states' rights. John C. Calhoun built upon the Madison's interpretation to formulate South Carolina's nullification theory invoked in 1833 to nullify the 1828 Tariff of Abominations. Calhoun argued that the tariff was not uniform in terms of geographic economic impact and therefore unconstitutional. In Calhoun's analysis, only a state had final authority to judge the constitutionality of a Federal law within its borders, not the Supreme Court. All states could only be forced to conform to such a law by passing a new amendment specifically making it constitutional. Southern statesmen tried to work out a middle ground that would incorporate Calhoun's philosophy

---

[105] Philip Leigh, *Civil War Chat*, "Differences between U.S. and Confederate Constitutions, Available: https://tinyurl.com/yd7dfk9j, [Accessed: June 20, 2020]

CAUSES OF THE CIVIL WAR

without neutering the Confederacy's Supreme Court, but the country collapsed at Appomattox before they completed their work.

Therefore, contrary to the presumption that the Civil War was all about slavery, the constitutional provisions noted above show that the Confederacy's founders had big misgivings about the powers of the Central Government. The stipulations also disclose that states' rights were one way Southerners intended to limit such powers. Thus, historians presently arguing that Southerners only mentioned states' rights as a war issue after the South lost the war are wrong. The Confederate Constitution undeniably shows that such rights had been a major consideration from the beginning.[106]

Although not attending the constitutional convention, Jefferson Davis was elected President of the provisional government on February 9, 1861 and was inaugurated on 18 February. During his inaugural address he stated that the Confederacy wanted to be at peace with all nations, including the United States. He also announced a desire to promote "the freest trade" possible thereby implying an intent to adopt low tariffs and competitive navigation laws to replace those that had allowed the Northeastern states to dominate the antebellum Southern costal trade. The provisional Congress formed six cabinet positions; state, war, navy, treasury, post office and justice. Davis filled each office with one man from each state except his home state of Mississippi. In November 1861 Confederate voters officially elected Davis as President, Alexander Stephens as Vice President, 105 congressmen and 26 senators to serve the permanent government, which succeeded the provisional government in February 1862. The provisional Congress had only

---

[106] Philip Leigh, *Abbeville Institute*, "Why No Confederate Supreme Court?" Available: https://tinyurl.com/y9bzdg7m, [Accessed: June 20, 2020]; Although James Madison would later claim that his Virginia Resolutions did not support Calhoun's construction of Nullification, historian Herbert Agar wrote that Madison's claim could not "be defended in logic." Herbert Agar, *The Price of Union*, 185.

one house and was composed of the men from the Confederacy's constitutional convention.[107]

Anticipating that the Confederacy must be prepared to defend her independence, Davis started selecting military leaders. On March 1, 1861 he chose former West Point Superintendent, Pierre G. T. Beauregard to take command in Charleston in order to assure that South Carolina did not hastily provoke a war by prematurely attacking Fort Sumter. Three days earlier Davis chose three commissioners and sent them to Washington to meet with the Lincoln Administration in order to negotiate a peaceful settlement for all unresolved matters between the two countries. Foremost among such matters was the occupation of military facilities such as Fort Sumter.

Jefferson Davis

Although Lincoln had been inaugurated by the time the commissioners arrived, he refused to meet them as did Secretary of State William H. Seward. On 13 March they submitted a written request for diplomatic recognition to Seward. The secretary did not respond directly but utilized Supreme Court Justice John Campbell of Alabama as an intermediary. Although Seward made no reply to the recognition request, the commissioners received assurances through Campbell from Seward that Major Anderson would

---

[107] William C. Davis, *Jefferson Davis: The Man and His Hour*, (New York: HarperCollins, 1991), 303-13; Merton Coulter, *The Confederate States of America*, (Baton Rouge: LSU Press, 1959), 134

abandon Fort Sumter. Given Seward's office and status as a venerable Republican Party leader, they did not realize that the secretary was speaking only for himself, not Lincoln. Seward had mistaken President-elect Lincoln's four-month public silence for diffidence. He evidently presumed a duty to take responsibility for relations with the cotton states in his capacity secretary of state. That presumption would lead to complications, misunderstandings, and Civil War.[108]

[108] William C. Davis, *Jefferson Davis: The Man and His Hour*, 321-22; Merton Coulter, *The Confederate States of America*, 37; Kenneth Stampp, *And the War Came*, 273

CHAPTER 10: SECESSION CRISIS

WHEN LINCOLN MOVED into the White House on March 4, 1861 neither Congress nor the Washington Peace Conference had achieved a compromise. Two days earlier, both congressional chambers passed an amendment introduced by Ohio Congressman Thomas Corwin stipulating that Congress could never interfere with slavery in the states where it was legal. The proposed amendment was forwarded to the states for ratification. But even Lincoln recognized it was a meaningless gesture because it was redundant to the original Constitution. Congress already had no power to intrude. As a result, the seven cotton states considered themselves an independent Confederacy, no longer ruled by the United States. Conversely, Lincoln regarded them as a contiguous group of seven states temporarily controlled by an unlawful ring of dissidents. His challenge was to pacify, or smash, the cabal and bring the seven states back into the Union without provoking other states to secede. Davis's challenge was to remain at peace and entice as many other states as possible to join the Confederacy.

Republicans began by sheepishly abandoning a key plank in the 1860 Party platform. Three days before Lincoln took office the Republican-controlled Congress carved three new territories—Dakota, Nevada, and Colorado—out of previous and larger territories. Since the acts forming the new territories made no mention of slavery, they were technically open to slaveholders by default under the Dred Scott ruling. It was an indirect admission that popular sovereignty would stop the spread of slavery, for which Senator Douglas justifiably scolded Republicans for belatedly adopting. If they had dropped their no-slaves-in-any-territories policy six months earlier the Civil War may have been avoided. As matters stood, however, Lincoln felt compelled to focus on Fort Sumter rather than assume any blame for his Party's tardy endorsement of popular sovereignty.[109]

For him, the fort symbolized Federal power in the rebellious states. For Davis it signified an alien power within his domestic borders. Although the Federals still occupied Fort Pickens in Pensacola, Florida under a standstill agreement accepted by lame-duck Buchanan, Lincoln would absorb a serious prestige blow if he gave up Sumter without getting something substantial in return. By merely holding the forts, however, he would cause Davis to lose credibility, possibly to the point of inspiring the cotton states to return to the Union. Specifically, Davis's bid to join the community of nations would fail if he could not rid his country of a hostile power. If the Confederacy could not peaceably occupy Fort Sumter, it would be compelled to either capture it or repel any future reinforcing Union flotilla. Thus, if there was to be a war Lincoln could force Davis to fire the first shot by indefinitely provisioning Major Anderson's garrison.

The morning after his 4 March inauguration, Lincoln received a message from Anderson stating that Fort Sumter had enough provisions to last about six weeks. The major also warned that securing the fort might require 20,000 men, which was more than the total number of soldiers in Lincoln's standing army. Since the new President was overwhelmed by office-seekers he did not even discuss Sumter in his first cabinet meeting on 6 March, which was limited to introductory conversations. But Sumter was the chief topic in the 9 March meeting. By then General of the Army Winfield Scott had privately told the President that he agreed with Anderson's estimate about the number of troops required to hold the fort. If true, that would have made it impossible for Lincoln to

---

[109] J. G. Randall and David Donald, *The Civil War and Reconstruction*, 178-79

sustain Anderson's garrison. But other qualified observers were not as pessimistic as Scott. One was Postmaster General Montgomery Blair, a West Point graduate. His brother-in-law, Gustavus Fox, was a navy veteran who had been working on a plan under Buchanan to resupply the fort with vessels towed by light draft New York tugboats under cover of darkness.

William H. Seward

On 15 March Lincoln asked cabinet members to state in writing whether they thought an attempt should be made to re-supply Sumter, assuming it was feasible. Seward opposed it on the grounds that it would provoke Civil War. Most of the other six joined him. But Montgomery Blair backed his brother-in-law and Treasury Secretary Salmon P. Chase sided with Blair in a qualified approval, if the relief attempt was unlikely to provoke war. That same day, Seward met with Justice Campbell who volunteered that he would be sending an update letter to Jefferson Davis. In response to Campbell's question about what the Justice should say, Seward responded, "You may say that before that letter reaches him the telegraph will have informed him that Sumter will have been evacuated." Seward had not yet explained to Lincoln that he hoped to defuse the secession crisis by dragging it out without any shooting until the cotton states realized for themselves that their future was better if they voluntarily returned to the Union. He believed there was enough pro-Union sentiment in those states to yield such a result.[110]

Given the division in his cabinet, Lincoln did not presently reach a decision of his own. Privately, however, he concluded that evacuation "would be utterly ruinous" politically if he did not gain something of value by surrendering the fort. Faced with a seemingly impossible choice, he postponed action in order to collect more information. He sent Fox and private emissaries to Charleston. Fox returned more confident than ever that his resupply plan would work. Since he wanted to retain the element of surprise should Lincoln decide to proceed, Fox pretended to agree with Anderson's objections when the two discussed the plan in Charleston. The other emissaries returned to confirm that South Carolinians were inflexibly set upon Confederate independence. There was apparently little love remaining for the Union despite Lincoln's "mystic chords of memory" appeal in his inauguration speech.

On 29 March Lincoln called another cabinet meeting to consider the situations at Forts Sumter and Pickens. Only six of the seven secretaries were present, War Secretary Simon Cameron being absent. Seward continued to believe that any attempt to supply Fort Sumter would lead to war but opined that Pensacola's Fort Pickens should be held "at every cost" and the interior secretary agreed. Attorney General Bates agreed with Seward on Fort Pickens but offered no opinion on Sumter. The postmaster general, navy secretary and treasury secretary argued that Sumter should be re-supplied. Blair even threatened to resign if no attempt was made.

The reasons for the shift in cabinet sentiment have never been clarified but they probably reflected a growing realization that the Federal Union might collapse if the cotton states were allowed to circumvent United States tariffs. Fort Sumter had become more

---

[110] David Donald, *Lincoln*, 285-8; Maury Klein *Days of Defiance*, 334; Kenneth Stampp, *And the War Came*, 273-74

than a symbol. It was an armed facility usefully located in Charleston Harbor's main shipping channel where Federal authorities could force incoming vessels to stop and pay customs duties. Since Charleston was the largest Atlantic port in the seven-state Confederacy, that was no small matter. A 2 March *New York Evening Post* editorial underscored the point: "[E]ither the revenue from duties must be collected in the ports of the rebel states, or the ports must be closed to importations from abroad, is generally admitted. If neither of these things be done, our revenue laws are substantially repealed; the sources which supply our treasury will be dried up; we shall have no money to carry on the government; the nation will become bankrupt before the next crop of corn is ripe."

Lincoln's inaugural address also drew a line in the sand over revenue laws: "[T]here needs to be no bloodshed or violence, and there shall be none unless it be forced upon the national authority. The power confided to me will be used to hold, occupy, and possess the property and places belonging to the Government and to collect the duties and imposts; but beyond what may be necessary for these objects, there will be no invasion, no using of force against or among the people anywhere." Thus, Lincoln implied that he intended to use force to collect tariffs. After 29 March, it was no longer a mere implication but a daily growing probability. He was almost suggesting that the cotton states might pretend among themselves to have seceded, but they were going to pay tribute to Washington as a cost of pretending. The North had redefined the South's "coercion" argument into a more palatable expression for their purposes: "enforcement of the revenue laws."

Otto Eisenschiml suggested a second reason for the policy change after the 29 March cabinet meeting in his 1958 book, *Why the Civil War?* He theorized that Lincoln and Seward were prepared to give up Fort Sumter if they could secure Pensacola's Fort Pickens and gain something of value in exchange for giving up Sumter. Specifically, Lincoln hoped to persuade Virginia to adjourn their secession convention *sine die* thereby keeping the state in the Union. He reasoned, probably correctly, that if Virginia remained Union-loyal few of the remaining slave states would join the seven-state Confederacy even in the event of hostilities. Both men were aware that on 12 March General Scott had sent reinforcements to Fort Pickens, which were expected to arrive any day. After the 29 March cabinet meeting, the pair developed a secret plan to more substantially reinforce Fort Pickens with soldiers and the USS *Powhatan,* a powerful warship. The President authorized the mission that same day but intentionally did not notify Navy Secretary Gideon Welles because Seward warned that the Navy Department had many Southern sympathizers.

On 31 March Scott's reinforcements arrived at Pensacola but were denied access to the fort by the ranking naval officer locally.

USS *Powhatan*

He objected that he had no authorization directly from the Navy Department to allow reinforcements for the fort. Unaware of the problem in Pensacola, on 1 April Lincoln used ordinary channels to authorize a second mission, to Sumter this time. When Navy Secretary Gideon Welles stipulated that he wanted the USS *Powhatan* to join the Sumter expedition he unexpectedly learned that the ship had a conflicting assignment. Welles asked the President for clarification that very evening, but Lincoln merely told him the *Powhatan* was unavailable.

Not until 6 April did Lincoln learn that Scott's reinforcements for Fort Pickens remained aboard ship off Pensacola due to the chain-of-command snafu noted above. He immediately sent a navy officer to Pensacola by train to get the troops ashore. Simultaneously, he put Gustavus Fox in charge of the Sumter expedition.

On, or about, 20 March, Lincoln had sent an invitation for George W. Summers, a leading Unionist member of Virginia's Secession Convention, to confer at the White House. After Summers hesitated, Lincoln sent a messenger to Richmond on 2 April who returned on 4 April with John Baldwin, another Virginia Convention Unionist. When Lincoln stated that he would abandon Sumter if the Virginia Convention would permanently adjourn, Baldwin was unreceptive. The Virginian added that any hostilities intended to coerce the cotton states back into the Union would likely cause his state to secede. Thereafter Lincoln concluded that his chances of gaining anything significant by vacating Sumter were fading away. Nonetheless, the secret Seward-Lincoln expedition left New York for Pensacola on 6 April. The ships for Fox's Sumter flotilla departed New York over three days, 8-10 of April.

During the eight days between 29 March and 6 April, Seward continued to search for a way to persuade Lincoln to avoid a confrontation at Fort Sumter, preferably by abandoning it. One option was to pick a fight with Spain in order to annex Cuba. That, he reasoned, would motivate the cotton states to return because they would not want the U.S.A. to take control of the island's slave-based economy. The Confederacy, felt Seward, likely wanted Cuba for themselves. Due to his earlier promises to the Confederate envoys, he was anxious to convince Lincoln to abandon Sumter and instead focus on securing Fort Pickens. On 30 March an increasingly skeptical Justice Campbell visited Seward for an update. The secretary promised to reply on April Fool's Day. When

Campbell returned on 1 April he asked, "Would Sumter be evacuated?" Seward requested a moment's time to visit Lincoln. Upon returning he gave Campbell a note that read, "I am satisfied the Government will not undertake to supply Fort Sumter without giving notice to [South Carolina] Gov. Pickens."[111]

Today's scholars don't know whether Lincoln told Seward that he had decided to hold onto Sumter before Seward replied to Campbell. Instead they know that the President prepared a memorandum that same day stating his intent to hold Sumter and rejecting the secretary's Cuba initiative. Nevertheless, later public remarks by Lincoln suggest that Eisenschiml's theory of a secret agreement between Lincoln and Seward to abandon Sumter was true. Specifically, when Congress reconvened on 4 July (directed by Lincoln on 15 April) the President told its members that he could have evacuated Sumter up to 6 April, but could not thereafter because that's when he learned the reinforcements sent to Pensacola's Fort Pickens had not been allowed to go ashore. Since he did not learn that Scott's reinforcements for Pickens were permitted to enter the fort until 12 April, his hands were tied on Sumter. He could not give up Sumter without knowing that he could hold onto Pickens. Except for the chain-of-command hitch that kept Scott's reinforcements idle off Pensacola for six days, Lincoln could have evacuated Sumter thereby avoiding the hostilities that started the war.

Whatever the true back stair intrigues at the White House, the Confederates concluded that Seward's 1 April note signified a major change. The next day Confederate War Secretary LeRoy Walker told General Beauregard at Charleston to prevent any reinforcement of

---

[111] David Donald, *Lincoln*, 287-88; Maury Klein, *Days of Defiance*, 333-34, 358, 370; Abraham Lincoln, "First Inaugural Address," (March 4, 1861) Available: https://tinyurl.com/y9ac6tp5 [Accessed: July, 2020]; Charles Adams, *When In the Course of Human Events*, 24; Otto Eisenschiml, *Why the Civil War?*, (Indianapolis, In.: Bobbs-Merrill, 1958), 23-26, 39, 45

Sumter. On 5 April his Washington envoys wired Davis, "An important move requiring a formidable military and naval force is certainly on foot." Here's what happened.[112]

On 8 April the *New York Tribune* correctly reported that Lincoln had sent messengers to inform South Carolina Governor Pickens that a resupply vessel was headed for Sumter. It would not add soldiers or weapons to the fort unless fired upon. That same day Seward formally rejected the Confederacy's 13 March request for diplomatic recognition. The newspaper article and diplomatic recognition rebuff prompted Justice Campbell to ask Seward for yet another update. Seward replied with an undated and unsigned note: "Faith as to Sumter fully kept; wait and see; other suggestions received and will be considered."

Campbell puzzled over the response. He did not know if Seward was pledging that the fort would be evacuated, or merely that Governor Pickens would be notified in advance of a resupply attempt, which officially happened that very day. The envoys were unaware that on 1 April Seward had sent a position paper to the President explaining why the secretary thought it wise to abandon Sumter and make common cause with the South against Spain. As noted, ultimately Lincoln responded by rejecting the suggestions. He also clarified, that as President, he would determine Administration policy toward the cotton states, not Seward. Whatever backstage maneuvers might have happened within Lincoln's cabinet, Campbell and the Confederate envoys concluded that a hostile movement was underway.[113]

As word leaked out that Lincoln was sending a relief expedition to Sumter most Northerners believed it would provoke Civil War.

---

[112] Maury Klein, *Days of Defiance*, 371; Ludwell Johnson, "Fort Sumter and Confederate Diplomacy," *The Journal of Southern History,* v. 26, n. 4, (November 1960), 465; Kenneth Stampp, *And the War Came*, 282-84

[113] Maury Klein, *Days of Defiance*, 377, 392-93

Historian Kenneth Stampp wrote, "The whole North assumed in advance that the expedition meant war; and, on April 4 . . . state governors returned from an invited conference with the President to speed their war preparations. Early in April Lincoln strove to organize the defenses of Washington. On April 9 he warned Pennsylvania's Governor Curtin of the necessity of being ready . . . John G. Nicolay and John Hay, the President's private secretaries, believed it was 'reasonably certain' that he expected hostilities to ensue. And when news of the attack arrived, he was neither surprised nor excited."

The specific message that Lincoln's courier gave Governor Pickens on 8 April read: "I am directed by the President of the United States to notify you to expect an attempt will be made to supply Fort Sumter with provision only; and that, if such attempt be not resisted, no effort to throw in men, arms or ammunition will be made without further notice, or in case of attack upon the fort." When Pickens asked if he might send a reply, the messenger said he was not authorized to accept one and left.

Pickens next seized Sumter's outgoing mailbag on 9 April. He opened three letters including one from Anderson to Washington written after the major had learned that a relief force was on its way. In part, it warned: "A movement made now, when the South has been erroneously informed that none will be attempted, would produce disastrous results throughout the country." Thus, Fox's deception when the two men discussed the plan during his visit to Charleston convinced Anderson that a rescue would not be attempted. Governor Pickens sent Anderson's letter to President Davis.

Jefferson Davis called a cabinet meeting on the same day to consider the Sumter situation. Eager to gain European diplomatic recognition, he argued that General Beauregard should capture the fort. All cabinet members agreed except Secretary of State Robert Toombs. Davis decided to continue the meeting the next day when the balance scale remained six-to-one against Toombs. According to a postbellum recollection by War Secretary Walker, Toombs spoke candidly: "The firing on that fort will inaugurate a civil war greater than any the world has yet seen. . . Mr. President, at this time it is suicide . . . It is unnecessary; it puts us in the wrong; it is fatal." Nevertheless, Davis had War Secretary Walker telegraph Beauregard to open fire if Sumter would not surrender.

At four o'clock on the afternoon of 11 April, Beauregard's negotiators met with Major Anderson at Fort Sumter and asked him to evacuate. He declined but added that the garrison would be starved out within a few days. Beauregard forwarded Anderson's remark to Davis and held fire until he got a reply. At Davis's instruction, the general sent negotiators back to Anderson to ask if he would specify a date on which he would abandon the fort for want of provisions and promise not to fire on Confederates. Anderson estimated he would withdraw on 15 April. Since the Confederates realized that Fox's Union squadron was already nearby, the reply was unsatisfactory. Beauregard next gave notice that he would commence a bombardment, which started at four o'clock on the morning of 12 April. Sumter surrendered the following day. There were no casualties on either side.

Due to foul weather, one of Fox's tugboats never left New York and the other two returned to the harbor. The remaining squadron consisted of one warship, one armed revenue cutter and a chartered merchant steamer. Although watching Beauregard's bombardment from the mouth of Charleston Harbor, Fox concluded it was too dangerous to join the fight without a local harbor pilot to avoid underwater hazards. He also hesitated because he was futilely awaiting the arrival of the USS *Powhatan* without realizing that she had been sent to Pensacola. In the end, the only concrete service of Fox's expedition was to evacuate Sumter's surrendered garrison.[114]

---

[114] *Ibid.*: 390-92, 397, 399; Bruce Catton *The Coming Fury*, 320; William Marvel, *Mr. Lincoln Goes to War*, (Boston: Houghton-Mifflin, 2006), 23; Kenneth Stampp, *And the*

In another sense, however, Fox may have accomplished much more. Lincoln's private secretaries, Nicolay and Hay, believed that the President regarded the success or failure of Fox's voyage as "a question of minor importance." Lincoln, they concluded, was determined "that the rebellion should be put in the wrong" so that the Confederates "would not be able to convince the World that he had begun the civil war." When Fox complained on 4 April that Sumter's food shortage did not give his mission enough time to succeed, Lincoln replied, "You will best fulfill your duty to your country by making the attempt." After Sumter surrendered, Lincoln wrote Fox a reassuring letter: "You and I both anticipated that the cause of the country would be advanced by making the attempt to provision Fort Sumter even if it should fail; and it is no small consolation now to feel that our anticipation is justified by the result." Several months later he repeated the point to Illinois Senator Orville Browning and added that Sumter's surrender "did more service" than if it had been held.[115]

Fort Sumter's capitulation galvanized and polarized Americans, North and South, as never before. Public displays of belligerence to defend against Northern invasion and coercion in the South were matched by similar spectacles in the North to put-down Southern rebellion. On 15 April Lincoln called upon the states outside the seven-state Confederacy to provide 75,000 militia *pro rata* to be put into national service in order to suppress the Confederate rebellion and collect tariffs within its borders. He also called for Congress to assemble in a special session, which he scheduled for three months later on July 4, 1861. Critics have long suspected that the delay was intended to enable the President to irrevocably begin a Civil War

---

War Came, 284; Ludwell Johnson, "Fort Sumter and Confederate Diplomacy," *The Journal of Southern History*, v. 26, n. 4, (November 1960), 476

[115] Kenneth Stampp, *And the War Came*, 284-85

that the legislative branch would be powerless to stop by the time it reconvened.

Otto Eisenschiml suggests that Lincoln was willing to run the risk of war because he expected that it would be a brief one. Perhaps it was a common opinion based upon post-Sumter press editorials and articles. Horace Greeley's *New York Tribune* opined, "The nations of Europe may rest assured that Jeff. Davis & Co. will be swinging from the battlements at Washington . . . by the 4th of July." The *New York Times* wrote, "Let us make quick work . . . A strong active 'pull together' will do our work . . . in thirty days. The *Philadelphia Press* said, "no man of sense would, for a moment, doubt that this much-ado-about-nothing could end in a month." The *Cincinnati Commercial* editorialized, "the rebellion will be crushed out before the [4 July] assemblage of Congress—no doubt of it." The *Chicago Tribune* boasted, "Let the East get out of the way . . . We can fight the battle, and successfully, within two or three months at the furthest. Illinois can whip the South by herself."[116]

Meanwhile, Lincoln assumed dictatorial powers. Within days of Sumter's surrender he blockaded Southern ports, a move internationally recognized as an act of war. He started suspending *habeas corpus* less than two weeks later. Thus, political opponents, and those merely speaking publicly against the war, could be jailed indefinitely without being charged with a crime. A few weeks thereafter he started shutting down newspapers. On 3 May he again ignored Congress's prerogative by calling for even more troops, this time for three-year enlistments. By the time Congress convened, Lincoln's army was developing plans to invade Virginia. Elected representatives had little to do but rubber-stamp his war measures or run the risk of being vilified as unpatriotic, or even traitors. They were scared of political retaliation from the executive branch. The Constitution was hanging by a thread.

---

[116] Otto Eisenschiml, *Why the Civil War?*, 114

Governors from seven of the eight remaining slave states rejected the militia call, generally citing it as an illegal coercion of sovereign members of America's constitutional compact. Maryland's governor met with Lincoln to explain that he wanted weapons to arm his militia but only if her troops were never deployed beyond her borders. His purpose was to use the men to deal with in-state violence that might occur during the present crisis. He told Lincoln that he opposed using Federal military force against any state.[117]

Virginia, North Carolina, Tennessee and Arkansas joined the Confederacy between 7 May and 2 July. Missouri was kept in the Union by prompt military coercion in the form of attacks against the state militia (renamed the State Guard) by Federal troops stationed in St. Louis. Maryland was kept out when Lincoln directed military forces to arrest suspected secessionist members of the General Assembly travelling to a special session where secession was to be considered at Frederick on 17 September. Kentucky settled upon a policy of "armed neutrality" that barred either Federal or Confederate troops from the state. She eventually tipped toward the Union when Confederate Major General Leonidas Polk seized Columbus, Kentucky on 3 September. Delaware excused herself from answering Lincoln's call by explaining she had no militia but thereafter remained Union-loyal. Late in 1861 a Missouri rump legislature and Kentucky pro-Confederate convention put their states in the Confederacy with shadow governments, but Southern forces never controlled either state.

The battle lines had been drawn.

---

[117] Leslie R. Tucker, *Major General Isaac Ridgeway Trimble,* (Jefferson, N.C.: McFarland, 2005), 104-05; Bruce Catton, *The Coming Fury,* 327; Charles Adams, *When In the Course of Human Events,* 39

CHAPTER 11: PRESERVING THE UNION

AS EXPLAINED IN CHAPTER eight, today's scholars typically rely upon statements supporting slavery in the secession *Declarations of Causes* issued by most of the cotton states to conclude that the Southerner's defense of slavery caused the Civil War. If, for purposes of argument, it is admitted that the first seven states that joined the Confederacy seceded chiefly to protect slavery, it still does not logically follow that secession caused the war. That false equivalency is too often unconsciously assumed. In truth, the North could have evacuated Fort Sumter and let the cotton states leave the Union in peace. Everyone realized that Southerners had no intent to overthrow the Washington government. They just wanted a government of their own.

Historian William Marvel challenges the presumed secession-means-war equivalency. He argues that historians who merely narrate events as they actually happened can be left with "an unintentionally narrow perspective through a reluctance to address alternatives available to the [historical] participants." That tendency has led to a "near-unanimous agreement that the conflict yielded the most desirable results, and the principal beneficiary has been Abraham Lincoln." By arrogating extraordinary authority to the executive branch, "he created precedents that permanently jeopardized the liberty the constitution promised to all Americans . . . [inadequately] . . . offset by the freedoms his actions would incidentally provide for the enslaved minority."

The byproduct of the war, emancipation, has come to dominant the memory of the conflict so thoroughly, that no contradiction now seems apparent in the establishment of federal power to impose universal, involuntary military service as a method for ending involuntary servitude.

Let us suppose there were no ground for secession. If it was unconstitutional, did the opponents of secession have the right to combat it with equally unconstitutional measures? Was the President's subsequent response any less illegal than the actions of the secession conventions merely because his excesses followed theirs chronologically? . . . Was the preservation of the national borders worth the precedent of the chief executive unilaterally initiating warfare, arbitrarily suspending civil liberties, jailing thousands on suspicion or political whim, using the military to manipulate elections and even overthrow the legitimate governments of states? . . . Did the permanent weakening of America's best protections against tyranny not exceed the violence done to the Constitution by the secession of seven states, and might that fundamental document have survived in firmer health with the remaining twenty-seven states adhering to it all the more strictly?

For that matter would bifurcation of the United States have been worse than the war waged to prevent it? The instinctive reply (after requisite reference to the abolition of slavery) asserts that the precedent of secession would have led to further divisions, until the former nation had been thoroughly Balkanized . . . Yet the very choice of the pejorative term "Balkanized," which is often employed in that argument, carries with it an assumption that a continent of smaller republics would not have been preferable. . . [and fails to appreciate that] . . . unopposed secession in 1861 ought, at least initially, to have eased the conflict between the sections—rather than aggravating it.

It was Lincoln, however, who finally eschewed diplomacy and sparked a confrontation when he fully understood the volatility of the situation. . . Lincoln's misjudgments of 1861 are overshadowed in the public memory by the results of 1865, which seem to validate his earlier decisions.

Northerners might have allowed the Southern tier of states to withdraw and form their own government. . . but instead they made . . . the usual choice, pitting their populations against one another in a devastating collision. . . It might be added that they [both sides] should also be judged by the moral standards of their own time, rather than by the values of future generations.[118]

Notwithstanding Marvel's thought-provoking interrogatories, identifying the cause of the Civil War requires an investigation into *why* the North chose to force the cotton states back into the Union. A good place to start is to study the joint legislative resolutions issued by ten of the free states explaining their objections to cotton state secessions. The first of the ten was New York's on January 14, 1861. That was five days after South Carolina fired upon the *Star of the West* as discussed in chapter eight. Aside from fulminating about Southern "treason" New Yorkers wrote that they "were profoundly impressed with the value of the republic and determined to preserve it unimpaired." Apart from a general anger at Southern "treason," the other nine states also expressed appreciation for the value of the Federal Union and their intent to preserve it. Minnesotans additionally felt that unrestricted access to New Orleans was vital to their economy. New Jersey's resolution urged compromise and suggested Crittenden's plan. None of the ten stated any wish to abolish slavery. To the contrary, some emphasized they had no desire to interfere with slavery in the states where it was then legal.

The resolutions were among the earliest formal statements from Northerners indicating their resolve to make war in order to

---

[118] William Marvel, *Mr. Lincoln Goes to War*, xii-xvii

preserve the Union. Similarly, in his 4 March first inaugural address, President Lincoln optimistically tried to evoke among Southerners, "The mystic chords of memory" that he hoped would "yet swell the chorus of the Union." Less than five months later after the Battle of First Manassas, the U.S. Congress almost unanimously adopted a joint resolution stating that their only objective in the war was to reunify the country, not to free the slaves.[119]

Gore Vidal, who wrote a popular and well-researched novel about Lincoln as part of his American Chronicles, questioned the nobility vouchsafed to the "preserve the Union" mantra in an interview: "I always thought Lincoln was wrong. I always thought the South had every right to go. If Lincoln had a high moral purpose—which has now been invented for him, posthumously, the abolition of slavery—I'd say, well it's illegal but it's morally worthy." At the time, however, Lincoln's motivations were to preserve the Union and centralize power in Washington. "Why," Vidal adds, "kill 600,000 young men for *a notion* of the Union, which nobody had thought much of before then?"[120]

Like nearly all of his academic colleagues, historian Gary Gallagher agrees that slavery caused the war. Unlike them, however, he has observed that: "Students and adults interested in the Civil War are reluctant to believe that anyone would risk life or fortune for something as abstract as *the Union.*" In truth, their reaction is common sense. The typical 1860 American seldom traveled beyond the borders of his state. If he paid taxes, he paid them to his state, usually in the form of property or poll taxes. He usually only paid Federal taxes indirectly when he purchased

---

[119] Philip Leigh, "Northern Response to Southern Secession," *Civil War Chat Blog,* Available: https://tinyurl.com/y7runqtz [Accessed: June 29, 2020] The ten free state resolutions were for Minnesota, Wisconsin, Indiana, Michigan, Ohio, Pennsylvania, Maine, Massachusetts, New Jersey, and New York; David Donald, *Lincoln,* 307-08

[120] Gore Vidal, *Lecture to the National Press Club* (March 19, 1988) Available: https://www.c-span.org/video/?1708-1/proposals-improve-us-government [Accessed: June 30, 2020]

imported goods after customs duties had already been built into the purchase price. Typically, his loyalty was to his state first and only secondarily to the Central Government.[121]

Even Gallagher concedes that economic concerns dominated the thoughts of the average 1860 American. As always, farmers worried about weather, pests, and market prices. Merchants focused on goods and consumers while bankers focused on loans and economic outlook. A Midwestern farmer, John Young, who maintained a personal journal reviewed the preceding year in his December 31, 1859 entry. He wrote about farm products, the weather, market prices, and his family's health. Although he was a Republican, he didn't mention anything about John Brown's attempted slave uprising, debates about slavery expansion, or other political matters. Only after secession became a reality in South Carolina on December 20, 1860, did Northerners begin to commonly express a love for the Union as in the free state resolutions noted above.[122]

In his latest Civil War book, *Lincoln's Mercenaries,* Marvel reveals that a substantial majority of white Union soldiers came from poor families even during the first wave of patriotism that followed Sumter's surrender. Statistics compiled by the University of Minnesota for the free states from the 1860 census disclose that 70% of soldiers during 1861 came from households in the bottom half of family wealth in their respective states. That ratio generally remained at 70% until the last year of the war (1864-65) when the below-median family wealth statistic dropped to 62%. Although the South's export engine recovered quickly from the 1857 financial panic, economic weakness lingered in the North. As winter ended in 1861 Northern newspapers reported large numbers of unemployed, partly because the cotton state secession triggered another downturn. Marvel writes, "Abundant and varied evidence

[121] Gary Gallagher, *The Union War,* (Cambridge: Harvard University Press, 2011), 3
[122] Gary Gallagher, *The Union War*, 44-45

reveals hundreds of thousands of destitute men scattered across the United States early in 1861." Regarding enlistments at the start of the war in April 1861 he adds, "the desire for economic relief, an employment opportunity, or a financial windfall often provided the initial impetus or overriding motive [for volunteering]."

Marvel's analysis is significant because it is based upon data as opposed selective quotations from diaries and letters. Unlike statistics, such quotes can be cherry-picked. Chandra Manning's theme of anti-slavery sentiment among Union soldiers in *What This Cruel War is Over* might be one example. Perhaps because he was not a soldier, or perhaps because it does not fit her agenda, the book fails to quote George Templeton Strong's famous journal: "We northerners object to slavery on grounds of political economy, not ethics."

Although Marvel has no data on the economic status of Confederate soldiers, Joseph Glatthaar's analysis of Robert E. Lee's army concludes that a larger share of the South's soldiers came from wealthy families as compared to Northern armies, perhaps because of the Southern aristocrat's tradition of *noblesse oblige*. Marvel also has no data on black enlistments into United States Colored Troops (USCT) units, although it seems logical that destitute ex-slaves had a powerful economic incentive to earn a regular salary as well as a motive to end slavery. The concentration camps for ex-slaves that emerged across the Union-occupied parts of the South were notoriously impoverished and disease ridden. Most able-bodied black males in such camps with no regular employment were good candidates for USCT enlistment.[123]

---

[123] William Marvel, *Lincoln's Mercenaries*, (Baton Rouge: LSU Press, 2018), xii, xiv, 24; "The Civil War Era," *Columbia University and Slavery,* Available: https://tinyurl.com/y7a6cp7t [Accessed: July 1, 2020]; Concentration camps were typically known as contraband camps during the Civil War because escaped slaves were termed contraband in order to deny an obligation to return them to their owners.

Lincoln's Mercenaries provides only some of the most recently discovered evidence that the Northern soldier's motive to "preserve the Union" reflected the regional desire to avoid the economic consequences of disunion. A truncated Union separated from its Southern states would face three economic problems.

First, it could not hope to maintain a favorable international balance of payments over the long run. The South accounted for about 71% of America's domestic product exports in 1859 and cotton alone represented 58%. Thus, without the South's export engine America might become a perpetual debtor nation forever at the mercy of its stronger trading partners that would deplete her gold reserves in order to settle the resulting trade imbalances. Domestic gold discoveries in California and elsewhere could only temporarily mask such consequences.[124]

Second, since the Confederate constitution outlawed protective tariffs her lower duties would confront the remaining states of the Union with two problems. First, tariff revenues would shrink. Articles imported into the Confederacy would divert the applicable import duties from the North to the South. Since tariffs represented ninety percent of all Federal taxes such a drop would significantly impact the Federal Government's finances. Second, and more important, a low Confederate tariff would cause Southerners to buy manufactured goods from Europe as opposed to the Northern states where prices were inflated by deterrence tariffs. Consequently, the market for Northern manufactured goods in the South might nearly vanish. In his 1860 book, *Southern Wealth and Northern Profits*, Thomas Kettell estimated that Northern

[124] Frank Owsley, *King Cotton Diplomacy*, (Chicago: University of Chicago Press, 1931), 13; DeBow's Review: Volume 30, Issues 1 – 4, (January – April, 1861), 364-65, Available: https://tinyurl.com/y8pe3w3b [Accessed: July 1, 2020]; "Growth of the Cotton Industry in America": https://www.sailsinc.org/durfee/earl2.pdf; Ronald Bailey, "The Other Side of Slavery," *Agricultural History*, v.68, n.2, (Spring 1994): 37, 44, 49

manufacturers annually sold $240 million of goods in the South. He also estimated that Northerners earned $63 million yearly in financial and insurance services on the South's international trade. Finally, he estimated Northerners sold imported goods valued at $106 million to the South thereby making the Southern market worth over $400 million annually to Northern suppliers.[125]

Third, an independent Confederacy would end the Northeast's near monopoly on coastal trade in the South. Their dominance dates to President George Washington's first Administration when New England's maritime industry persuaded Congress to pass prohibitive taxes on foreign vessels, as explained in chapter one. After the War of 1812 Congress passed the 1817 Navigation Act, which included a complete ban on foreign vessels from American coastal trade. It enabled Northeastern shippers to consolidate their position at home and internationally. By the end of 1818 America's coastal fleet was as big as her oceangoing fleet.[126]

It also gave birth to a shipping pattern termed the cotton triangle trade, which advantaged the Northeast. Early-and-mid nineteenth century Atlantic trade supremacy depended upon scheduled service. Such service began in 1817 with the emergence of New York's packet lines, so named because they carried diplomatic packets and mail. Since they received government mail subsidies, they were able to provide regular schedules whereas other ships would normally not depart until they had a full cargo load.

The packet lines enabled New York to create sizeable two-way cargo volumes, which the Southern ports were unable to do because cotton shipments were seasonal. Thus, New York's arriving international traffic included imported manufactured goods and immigrants. Typically, intercoastal trade left New York loaded with

---

[125] Thomas Kettell, *Southern Wealth and Northern Profits*, 74-75

[126] "Why the U.S. Embraced the Jones Act a Century Ago," *Bloomberg*, (October 16, 2017) Available: https://tinyurl.com/ybkmrbbq [Accessed: July 1, 2020]

goods, including imports, for Southern markets where they'd pick-up cotton bound for Europe. Since the 1817 law banned foreign vessels from America's costal trade, the cotton triangle enabled the Northeast's maritime industry to dominate the Atlantic trade such as New York-to-Charleston-to-Liverpool and back to New York.

By creating a three-cornered trade, New York pulled the commerce between the Southern ports and Europe out of its normal course and collected a heavy toll upon it. This trade might have otherwise become direct routes between Southern ports and Europe had New York not interposed. New York's income from triangle trade for financing, insurance, shipping, commissions and other services amounted to perhaps 40% of every dollar paid for Southern cotton. Moreover, in 1860 Southerners were paying Northern-owned vessels $36 million annually for intercoastal transportation. By the time Southern ports started offering transatlantic packet service in 1851 New York was far ahead in terms of departure-arrival frequencies and diversity of routes. America's international merchandise trade had increased from $120 million in 1830 to $670 million in 1860, yielding a 6% compound annual growth rate.[127]

To be sure, by 1860 New Orleans was the dominant port for cotton exports but most of it was shipped in American vessels owned by Northeasterners. Deep water vessels that took cotton from New Orleans to Liverpool would return to America by taking manufactured imports into New York. From New York, imports and other goods would be distributed to the South in the manner of the

[127] Robert Albion, *The Rise of New York Port: 1815-1860* (New York: Chas. Scribner & Sons, 1939), 95, K. Jack Bauer, *A Maritime History of the United States*, (Columbia: University of South Carolina Press,1988), 74-75; Doug Harper, "Slavery or Tariff?" *The American Civil War* Available: http://slavenorth.com/cw/economics.htm [Accessed: July 2, 2020]; Historical Statistics of the United States 1789 - 1945 (Washington: U.S. Government Printing Office, 1949), 247; "Maritime History," *Transportation Institute,* Available: https://tinyurl.com/ycr7ynyp [Accessed: July 2, 2020]; Charles Adams, *When In the Course of Human Events*, 27

cotton triangle, noted above. The seasonal nature of New Orleans exports combined with the Northeast's command of intercoastal shipping left the Crescent City unable to challenge New York's bilateral trade dominance. In the fiscal year ended June 30, 1859 New York collected about two-thirds of all import duties whereas New Orleans collected only about 4%.[128]

New Orleans Cotton

The method by which tariff differences contributed to the Civil War is often misunderstood. Those arguing against it focus on two points. First, since the eleven-state Confederacy had only 29% of America's antebellum population it is doubtful that they absorbed more than 30% of customs duties when they were part of the U.S.A. Moreover, 1860 tariffs totaled $54 million, which was only about

---

[128] Stephen R. Wise, *Lifeline of the Confederacy*, (Columbia: University of South Carolina Press, 1988), 228; David Cohn, *The Life and Times of King Cotton*, (New York: Oxford University Press, 1956), 84-85

1.2% of GDP. Second, the tariff rates in place at the start of the Civil War were the lowest since 1816.[129]

The above analysis has three flaws. First, it fails to consider that protective tariffs created near monopolies for Northern domestic manufactured goods. All three leading Northern manufacturing industries in 1860—cotton textiles, iron products and woolen textiles—benefitted from deterrence tariffs. All sold their products into the Southern markets, as well as other domestic regions. Second, other factors being equal, high tariffs caused the price of the South's agricultural products, or the quantity overseas buyers could afford to purchase, to drop by reducing the dollars importers could earn. They simultaneously increased the price of domestic and imported manufactured goods. Third, the maritime and other Northern trading interests worried that lower tariffs in the South would shift traffic to Southern ports and open the formerly closed Southern markets to foreign shipping. In 1860 American vessels carried 63% of imports and 70% of exports.[130]

Thus, a low tariff Southern Confederacy was an economic threat to a truncated Federal Union, particularly considering the North's growing expectations for economic hegemony as the South lost influence in the Government. About a month before Fort Sumter surrendered, the *Boston Transcript* concluded on March 18, 1861 that the South did not secede to protect slavery, but to become the North's economic competitor.

> Alleged grievances in regard to slavery were originally the causes for the separation of the cotton States, but the mask has been thrown off, and it is apparent that

---

[129] "What Was GDP Then? – Dropdown Menu," MeasuringWealth.com, Available: https://tinyurl.com/zrmljld [Accessed: July 2, 2020]; "U. S. Federal Government Revenues 1790-Present," *CRS Report of Congress*, Available: https://tinyurl.com/ybvbxoor [Accessed: July 2, 2020]

[130] "U. S. Federal Government Revenues 1790-Present," *CRS Report of Congress*, Available: https://tinyurl.com/ybvbxoor [Accessed: July 2, 2020]

the people of the seceding States are now for commercial independence. . . The merchants of New Orleans, Charleston, and Savannah are possessed with the idea that New York, Boston and Philadelphia may be shorn . . . of their mercantile greatness by a revenue system verging upon free trade. If the Southern Confederation is allowed to carry out a policy by which only a nominal duty is laid upon imports, no doubt the businesses of the chief Northern cities will be seriously injured.

The difference is so great between the tariff of the Union and that of the Confederacy that the entire Northwest [present day Midwest] must find it to their advantage to purchase imported goods at New Orleans rather than New York. In addition, Northern manufacturers will suffer from the increased importations resulting from low duties. . .[131]

Although Lincoln and his spokesmen avoided addressing the potential economic consequences of secession during his election campaign, Northerners started discussing them shortly after he became President-elect. More than a month before South Carolina started the secession trend and about two weeks after the election outcome was known, *The Boston Herald* concluded on November 12, 1860: "[Should the South secede] she will immediately form commercial alliances with European countries [that] . . . will help English manufacturing at the expense of New England. The first move the South would make would be to impose a heavy tax upon the manufacturers of the North, and an export tax on the cotton used by Northern manufacturers. In this way she would seek to cripple the North. The carrying trade, which is now done by American vessels, would be transferred to British ships." At least a

---

[131] Kenneth Stampp, *The Causes of the Civil War*, 92-93

part of the newspaper's prediction came true when the Confederacy levied an export cotton tax on May 21, 1861.[132]

On November 20, 1860 the Cleveland-based *National Daily Democrat* wrote, "it is said, the English Cabinet have . . . a Treaty which will allow the South to send their cotton free of duty to England, while English woolen and English cotton manufactured goods would be received free of duty into the cotton States. England would thus achieve the great object of her ambition, to have a monopoly of the raw cotton, and thus to strike a deadly blow at her great rival, the United States, and the result would be, that the cotton factories of the North—their best market cut off—the price of the raw cotton advanced, would be crippled if not entirely used up, and England would have the monopoly of that great trade."[133]

Ten days before South Carolina became the first state to secede on December 20, 1860 the *Chicago Daily News* wrote, "Let us . . . look dissolution [disunion] in the face: At one single blow our foreign commerce must be reduced to less than one-half what it now is. Our coastwise trade would pass into other hands. One-half of our shipping would lie idle at our wharves. We should lose our trade with the South, with all of its immense profits."

"Our manufactories would be in utter ruins. Let the South adopt the free-trade system, or that of a tariff for revenue [instead of deterrence], and these results would alike follow. If protection be wholly withdrawn from our labor, it could not compete . . . with the labor of Europe. We should be driven from the market, and millions of our people would be compelled to go out of employment."[134]

Since their city was America's dominant port, New Yorkers were particularly concerned about tariff circumvention. Specifically, they

---

[132] *Ibid.*: 91; John Schwab, *The Confederate States of America: 1861-1865 – A Financial and Industrial History* (New York: Charles Scribner & Sons, 1901), 240

[133] Charles Adams, *When In the Course of Human Events*, 25

[134] *Ibid.*, 23

feared that lower tariffs in the Confederacy would trigger extensive smuggling from the seceded states into the Federal Union. Concern became acute after President Buchanan signed the First Morrill Tariff on March 2, 1861, which widened the gap between Confederate tariffs and Federal tariffs.

Although Republicans tried to portray Morrill's as a revenue tariff, it had obvious deterrence components. One protected the iron products industry, which Pennsylvania delegates told Lincoln's 1860 nominating convention managers was crucial to winning their state. A second protective feature was a renewal of specific duties, to augment percentage rates thereby giving domestic producers added protection from declining prices as explained in chapter three. The feature was particularly selfish because Great Britain's growing manufacturing economy was steadily reducing unit production costs as volumes increased. Thus, specific duties triggered by minimum valuations not only protected Northern manufacturers against downward market price fluctuations but also against predictable price declines enabled by Britain's growing and sophisticated factory economy.

Thus, on 12 March the *New York Evening Post* wrote, "Allow railroad iron to be entered at Savannah with a low duty of ten percent . . . and not an ounce would be imported at New York. . . The whole country would be given up to an immense system of smuggling." Fifteen days later the *Post* reprinted an article from the St. Louis *Missouri Republican*: "Every day our importers of foreign merchandise are receiving, by way of New Orleans, very considerable quantities of goods duty free . . . If this thing is to become permanent there will be an entire revolution in the course of trade and New York will suffer terribly."[135]

By focusing their remarks on *ad valorem* percentages instead of specific fees, Republicans tried to divert attention from the

---

[135] Kenneth Stampp, *And the War Came,* 233-34

protective features of the First Morrill tariff. They deceptively claimed it was a revenue tariff designed to fill the Federal budget deficit that followed the 1857 financial panic. They long had the votes in the House of Representatives to pass the Morrill bill, which happened on May 10, 1860, six months before Lincoln was elected President. But they had to wait almost a year to get it through the Senate, which was accomplished only after the seven cotton states seceded and their senators resigned.

The House vote especially underscored the sectional differences. Only one congressman from the eleven states that would form the Confederacy voted in favor of the Morrill bill and thirty-nine voted against it. In contrast ninety-seven free-state congressmen voted for it and only fifteen against it. The lopsided House vote in favor of the bill demonstrated that sectional differences regarding protective tariffs were at least as obvious as were differences over slavery.[136]

One reason Southerners opposed Morrill's bill was its potential to provoke Great Britain's cotton textile industry to seek feedstock from other countries such as Egypt, Brazil, and India instead of the American South. Since America typically bought 40% of British exports, Morrill's higher tariffs would make it more difficult for the British to competitively sell manufactured goods to America. They would, therefore, have fewer dollars to pay for purchases of American cotton. Although soon-to-be-implemented war measures such as the Southern embargo and Northern blockade also motivated Europeans to find other cotton sources, the Morrill Tariff alone was sufficient incentive even if the Southern states had not seceded. When New York businessman August Belmont met with Prime Minister Lord Palmerston shortly after the Sumter crisis,

[136] "House Vote Number 151 in 1860 (36th Congress)," *Govtrack.us,* Available: https://tinyurl.com/trbzejx [Accessed: July 3, 2020]

Palmerston bluntly remarked: "We do not like slavery but want cotton and do not like your Morrill Tariff."[137]

During the initial year following the First Morrill Tariff, the average duty in the Federal Union was 26%. In contrast, the Confederacy initially adopted the rates of the 1857 Tariff, which averaged 17%. Even those initial Confederate rates were quickly lowered on major items such as cotton textiles and metal products from 24% to 15%, and in some cases 10%. The Confederate duty-free list included provisions, agricultural products, gunpowder, and ammunition, all tariffed in the North. It also exempted all ships carrying imports for the army. Due to the Lincoln's wartime blockade, however, Confederate customs collections were minimal.[138]

Nonetheless, the First Morrill Tariff sharpened the contrast between tariffs in the U.S.A. and C.S.A. Within a month, more than a hundred New York commercial importers, and a similar number in Boston, informed customs collectors that they would not pay the Morrill fees unless the fees were also collected in the cotton states. At the very time in late March when Lincoln was trying to decide whether to resupply Sumter, a team of New York merchants visited the White House. Afterward a Washington newspaperman reported that the tariff differential was their main topic. He added, "it is a singular fact that merchants who, two months ago were fiercely shouting 'no coercion' now are for anything rather than inaction." Historian Charles Adams concludes that Northern merchants "now saw that there was only one course for them. They had prospered

---

[137] Howard Jones, *Blue and Gray Diplomacy* (Chapel Hill: University of North Carolina Press, 2010), 62; Amanda Foreman, *A World on Fire,* (New York: Random House, 2010), 68

[138] John Schwab, *The Confederate States of America: 1861-1865 – A Financial and Industrial History*; U. S. Department of Commerce, "Historical Statistics of the United States: Colonial Times to 1970: Part 2," 885; U. S. Federal Government Revenues 1790-Present CRS Report of Congress, Available: https://tinyurl.com/ybvbxoor [Accessed: July 2, 2020]

under the Union as one nation, and they now believed that prosperity would continue only if the United States was maintained as one nation. They had no choice but to support Lincoln and his policy of preserving the Union. Better to pay for armed conflict now than suffer prolonged economic disaster in a losing trade war."[139]

While modern historians readily criticize the so-called Slavocracy for geographic ambitions they seldom admit Northerners had imperialistic tendencies of their own. During the War of 1812 they twice invaded British North America (Canada) intent on annexation. Even though Southerners were largely responsible for the Mexican Cession, nearly all of its best lands were populated by Northerners who had initially objected to the Cession. New England had even threatened to secede over it. As explained in chapter ten, in March 1861 Secretary of State William Seward recommended that Lincoln go to war with Spain with the aim of annexing Cuba. On January 11, 1861 the Washington correspondent for the *New York Tribune* wrote, "Key West, the Tortugas, and Pensacola belong more . . . to the great maritime and commercial interests of the Free States . . . Those posts are in themselves alone of sufficient importance to create and justify a war, even a long and bloody war, should their possession be contested." Northerners who were that much intent on imperialism were not going to permit the Southern Confederacy to become a Western Hemisphere commercial rival without a fight.[140]

---

[139] Charles Adams, *When In the Course of Human Events*, 66, 70
[140] Kenneth Stampp, *And the War Came,* 227

CHAPTER 12: POSTBELLUM RESULTS

MOST MODERN HISTORIANS have a curious perspective on postbellum results as an indicator of wartime objectives. Specifically, they only accept such outcomes as indicators when the outcomes coincide to their preconceived understanding of Civil War causes. One example is the Thirteenth Amendment, which freed the slaves. Increasingly academic historians claim the Amendment was merely the formal postwar adoption of a prewar objective. After all, they argue, Lincoln said in his first inaugural: "One section of our country believes slavery is right and ought to be extended, while the other believes it is wrong and ought not to be extended." If slavery was "wrong," today's historians contend, then surely Lincoln or the Republican Party intended to end it someday. Predictably, however, they dismiss postbellum results that reveal the North was also seeking other outcomes, such as economic hegemony. Consider the case of tariffs.[141]

One of the most convincing clues that tariffs were a prime reason Northerners chose to fight a war rather than evacuate Fort Sumter and let the seven cotton states leave in peace is evident in America's postbellum tariffs. Through their Republican Party proxy, the winners of the war increased the tariff on dutiable items from an average of 19% on the eve of the Civil War to an average of 45% for fifty years thereafter. The increases were at the behest of politicians

---

[141] Ira Berlin, "Book Review: The Scorpion's Sting by James Oakes," *The Washington Post*, (May 30, 2014), Available: https://tinyurl.com/y8dwgyz8 [Accessed: July 10, 2020]

mostly from the regions north of the Ohio River and Mason Dixon Line. Some observers deny that high postbellum tariffs were a Northern wartime objective by explaining that they were needed as a way to pay-off the national debt accumulated during the war. There is, however, only limited truth in that argument.

President Woodrow Wilson

Although the national debt increased from $65 million in 1860 to $2.7 billion in 1865, the percent of Federal tax revenue obtained from tariffs dropped from 97% to 29% during the war. The decline resulted from the adoption of a number of internal taxes (taxes levied on people and businesses within America's borders) such as a temporary income tax and various excise taxes. Excise taxes had the biggest increases. Significantly, the Federal Government quickly cut wartime internal taxes after the Confederacy surrendered but kept tariffs high. That is the key point. As before the war, high tariffs benefitted the Northern economy but hurt the Southern economy. By 1872 tariff revenues had increased 150% from 1865, while excise taxes had dropped by 35%. Their relative revenue contributions had also reversed. In 1872 tariffs were 62% of the revenues while excise taxes were only 34%. By comparison, in 1865 tariffs were only 29% of revenue and excises taxes were 60%.[142]

---

[142] "U. S. Federal Government Revenues 1790-Present: 1975," *CRS Report of Congress*, Available: https://tinyurl.com/ybvbxoor [Accessed: May 17, 2020]

Tariff rates did not begin to drop until Democrat, and boyhood Southerner, Woodrow Wilson became president in 1913. Like most postbellum Southerners he felt that Federal Government finances were too dependent upon tariffs, which were economically regressive taxes similar to modern sales taxes. Even though Southerners had tried earlier to get an income-sensitive Federal tax adopted to partially replace tariff fees, the Supreme Court had ruled that such a tax was unconstitutional despite its temporary use during the Civil War. Thus, a postbellum income tax could not be adopted until the Sixteenth Amendment was ratified in 1913.

During Wilson's two-terms, tariffs dropped from 47% of Federal revenues in 1913 to 13% in 1921. When Republicans regained the White House in the Roaring Twenties, tariff rates sharply rebounded. They did not begin to decline until the Great Depression. America didn't fully become a free trade advocate until the 1947 General Agreement on Tariffs and Trade. By that date the manufacturing economies of the Northern states had no international competitors because World War II had destroyed the economies of Europe and Asia. Under such circumstances they welcomed the freest trade possible, since the other countries of the World had no other place to buy manufactured goods. It was Detroit's halcyon era.[143]

After reporting an approximate $1 billion deficit in 1865 the Federal budget had a 29-year-run of consecutive surpluses until 1893. Part of the surplus reduced the national debt. Starting in the late 1870s, however, the Republican Party increasingly used tariff collections to pay generous pensions to Union veterans. (Confederate veterans could only qualify for smaller pensions from their respective states.) During the first twelve years after the Civil War, Union veterans' pensions nearly doubled from $14 million to

---

[143] *Ibid.: The WTO and GAAT: A Principled History,* Available: https://tinyurl.com/y799uaou [Accessed: July 7, 2020]

$27 million in 1878. Over the next fifteen years ended in 1893 the pensions climbed nearly five-fold from $27 million to $157 million. At that point they accounted for 41% of the entire Federal budget. Disbursements did not peak until 1921 when they totaled $255 million annually.[144]

Union veterans were basically bribed to vote for high-tariff Republicans who told the vets that tariffs produced the tax revenues needed to pay their pensions. For almost a half century after the war only a single Democrat, Grover Cleveland, was elected President. Moreover, despite a nation-wide popular vote majority Cleveland lost his 1888 bid for a second consecutive term when Benjamin Harrison narrowly beat him in Indiana and New York where veterans supplied the Republican edge. The two states had 38,000 and 45,000 veterans receiving pensions respectively, yielding Harrison 2,300 and 13,000 respective vote majorities. Cleveland's defeat at the end of his first term interrupted Democrat efforts to reduce tariffs.[145]

Notwithstanding that the above episodes were twenty to thirty years after the Civil War, they were lingering practices of antebellum Republican principles which were put in place immediately upon entering the war. The lengthy era of high postbellum tariffs had the same detrimental impact on the South's economy as did antebellum deterrence tariffs. As a result, Europeans had even fewer dollars with which to buy Southern cotton thereby slashing demand for cotton exports as well as forcing cotton prices lower. The consequences lasted at least seventy years. When explaining a multiyear decline in cotton exports in 1935

---

[144] U. S. Department of Commerce, "Historical Statistics of the United States: Colonial Times to 1970: Part 2, 1104, 1148, 1149; Louis Hacker and Benjamin Kendrick, *The United States Since 1865* (Appleton-Century-Crofts, 1949), 88

[145] Jill Quadagno *The Transformation of Old Age Security* (Chicago: University of Chicago Press, 1988), 37, 42; Claudia Goldin and Frank Lewis, "Economic Costs of the Civil War," *Journal Economic History*, v. 35, n. 2 (June 1975): 304

Assistant Treasury Secretary Oscar Johnston wrote, "The major cause of the decline is the inability of foreign consumers to obtain American exchange [dollars.]" Southern farmers needed export markets, but Republicans gave them American tariffs that drove the South's export customers to seek sources from other countries that had lower tariffs.[146]

Similarly, most of today's Civil War historians erroneously ignore Northern prosperity during the Gilded Age as an indicator of a Northern wartime objective. Also, like the Republicans of the era, they fail to appreciate how deterrence tariffs created many of the notorious late nineteenth century monopolies. When Congress first challenged monopoly power with the 1890 Sherman Antitrust Act, they provided a remedy that targeted only the apparatus of monopoly instead of the cause. Policy makers evidently did not recall John C. Calhoun's warnings about the links between tariffs and domestic monopolies. Finally, in 1899 the president of New York based American Sugar Refining Company, which controlled 98% of the market through its still-famous *Domino* brand, provided convincing testimony to an industrial commission:

> The mother of all trusts is the customs tariff bill . . .
>
> [Production economies of scale] . . . in the same line of business are a great incentive to [trust] formation, but these bear a very insignificant proportion to the advantages granted in the way of protection under the customs tariff . . . It is the Government through its tariff laws, which plunders the people, and the trusts . . . are merely the machinery for doing it.[147]

Tariffs bred monopolies like swamps bred mosquitoes. The era's biggest, United States Steel, was deliberately formed to suppress competition. Even though steel could be produced more cheaply in

---

[146] David L. Cohn, *The Life and Times of King Cotton*, 238

[147] Byron W. Jolt, "The Relation of the Protective Tariffs to the Trusts," *Publications of the American Economic Association,* 3rd series, v.8, n. 1 (Feb. 1907): 213

America than in other countries, U.S. Steel sold products overseas at lower prices than domestically. Wire nails, for example, sold domestically at $2 per hundredweight, compared to $1.55 in Britain. The year after the Civil War ended, British railroad iron was priced at $32 a ton in Liverpool as compared to $80 in New York. The higher New York price was almost entirely due to protective tariffs for domestic producers. It was an obvious burden on impoverished Southerners desperate to rebuild their railroads destroyed during the Civil War. They were required to pay a premium of more than 100% for new rails, all for the benefit of already prosperous Northern producers.[148]

Similarly, as heir to the Northern wing of the Whig Party, Republicans favored the centralization of banking regulation and a national currency. Since no such currency existed until the wartime Legal Tender and National Banking Acts, no Party platform mentioned it until Lincoln's second nomination in May 1864. At that convention, however, Lincoln's Party adopted a platform plank declaring the use of a national currency (instead of gold) to be a patriotic duty. The National Banking Acts were a convenient arrangement for the established banks because they left the postbellum South ultimately dependent upon the remote banking centers of the Northeast. Consequently, as late as 1900 only 7% of the nation's bank capital was located in the former Confederate states. Lingering wartime regulations made it hard to open national banks in the South for five reasons.[149]

First, national bank capital requirements were beyond the means of poor Southerners. Second, such banks generally could not make mortgage loans, a loan type essential to the agrarian South. Third, national banks were restricted to a single branch, which was

---

[148] *Ibid.*, 217-18, 220; Ida Tarbell, *The Tariff in Our Times*, (Norwood, Mass.: Macmillan, 1911), 31

[149] William J. Cooper and Thomas Terrill *The American South: Volume 2* (Lanham, Md.: Rowman & Littlefield, 2009) 458

a handicap in the sparsely populated South. Fourth, even though state-chartered banks might offer mortgages and/or require less start-up capital, a 10% Federal tax on their banknotes burdened them with prohibitive operating costs. Fifth, the total value of national banknotes allowed to circulate throughout the country were nearly at their regulatory maximum by the time Southern bankers were able to apply for national charters. Congress refused to take action to pragmatically lift the limits until 1900. The result was a tendency to keep banking centered in the Northeast.[150]

Despite such obstacles, the postwar South remained the World's low-cost producer of cotton. In fact, Northerners perpetuated its low-cost status by forcing the region to replace slave labor with impoverished sharecroppers, white and black. New England cotton textile makers and their ecosystem benefitted from Southern poverty because it gave their factories an abundant supply of cheap feedstock. By winning the Civil War the North transformed the South into an internal colony to be perpetually exploited by the North. Historian David L. Cohn explains how that result was not accidental after the Republicans took control of the Federal Government:

> Industrial capitalism was now in the saddle. Industrial capitalists, through their Republican spokesmen, had captured the state and they used it to strengthen their economic position. While the war was being waged on the battlefields and through Negro emancipation, the victory had been made secure in Congress by the

---

[150] Richard Sylla "Federal Policy, Banking Market Structure, and Capital Mobilization in the United States, 1863 – 1913," *The Journal of Economic History,* v.29, n. 4 (Dec. 1969), 659, 663-664; John Hicks *Populist Revolt* (Minneapolis: University of Minnesota Press, 1931), 39-40; Paul Studenski and Herman Krooss *Financial History of the United States* (Beard Books, 2001) 154-55, 178; William J. Cooper and Thomas Terrill *The American South: Volume 2* 457-58, 460

passage of legislation having to do with tariffs, banking, public lands, railroads and labor.

Eastern industrialists, who were bent on reconstructing the country for their own benefit, wasted no time in moving to do so after the Southern delegation had left Congress. . .

[After the war] The agrarian South had been delivered over to non-agrarian interests and had become a satellite of the banking industrial Northeast. And the already burdened cotton farmers were to bear heavier burdens in the future. They could complain in vain. . . of railroad rates that crippled them, of gouging by trusts and combines operating in cottonseed oil, jute bagging, farm implements, and other adversities. They might work hard, live meanly, and die in poverty to pass on to [future generations] the apparently irrevocable estate of poverty.[151]

Similarly, the 1862 Pacific Railroad Act quickly ushered in a pattern of crony capitalism that continued long after the war, mainly for the benefit of states outside the former Confederacy. After years of debate concerning the route of a potentially subsidized railroad, Congress took advantage of the absent Southern representatives to select a Northern track from Omaha to Sacramento. Moreover, they gave it huge subsidies in both land and government guaranteed bonds.

Corporate officers of the Union Pacific and Central Pacific railroads that would operate the route siphoned-off most of the subsidies into their privately-owned construction companies that built the lines. Beneficiaries included the names of still-familiar Robber Barons such as Mark Hopkins, Leland Stanford, Collis Huntington, and Charles Crocker. The Union Pacific's construction company, Crédit Mobilier, even sold bargain-priced stock to both of

---

151 David Cohn *The Life and Times of King Cotton,* 147, 149-150

President Ulysses Grant's Vice Presidents and other Republican politicians. When Lincoln signed the bill, both railroads existed only on paper, yet they would receive unprecedented subsidies.

While the status of the ex-slaves started to transform during the war, so also did that of America's railroads. They evolved from multi-gage lines and wood-burning engines into standard gage lines and coal-burning engines. The makeover, however, inaugurated an era of corruption and state-assisted capital formation that would become alternately known as The Gilded Age, or The Great Barbecue. Only politically connected Northerners were invited. One of the Age's chief characteristics was private exploitation of public resources, especially land.

Despite wretched and stubborn poverty in the South, historians of the Gilded Age simply overlook the region and describe the period as a halcyon era for America. Matthew Josephson wrote, "The decade after the Civil War was on the whole an ingenious and light-hearted one." In writing of the industry moguls, he added: "The newly rich who had so quickly won to supreme power in the economic order enjoyed almost universal esteem for at least twenty years after the Civil War. Their glory was at its zenith; during this whole period, they literally sunned themselves in the affection of popular opinion."[152]

Although the Great Barbecue originated during the Civil War and became a national obsession immediately thereafter, it excluded Southerners and blacks. Railroads were eventually given nearly twice as much land (200 million acres) as contained within California's borders. From ratification of the U.S. Constitution in 1789 to the 1873 economic downturn, the Federal government invested $105 million in transportation facilities such as railroads, canals and ordinary roads but less than $5 million was deployed in the South. In 1873 over $80 million had been invested in the

---

[152] Matthew Josephson *The Robber Barons*, 145, 315

Northern transcontinental railroads and schemes during the preceding fifteen years.

After the grants to the Union Pacific and Central Pacific, Congress awarded enormous land tracts to three new

Chinese RR Workers

transcontinental lines; Santa Fe, Northern Pacific and Southern Pacific. None were owned by Southerners. Land grants for the Northern Pacific alone were equivalent to the size Missouri. When Pennsylvania business leaders Thomas Scott and Andrew Carnegie tried to organize subsidies in 1873 for a Southern network that would include a new transcontinental line to be called the Texas & Pacific, Congress told them the Great Barbecue was over.

While nearly all the ex-slaves remained in the South where they yearned for land, the Federal Government gave them none. From 1865 to 1873 less that 10% of all Federal public works spending was in the former Confederate states despite their greater need. In combination, New York and Massachusetts got more than twice as much as all the states in the former Confederacy.[153]

One of the Northerners' biggest wartime objectives was to gain control of the South so that they could soak-off her antebellum wealth. During the war Yankees even bought cotton from impoverished Southerners living in Union-occupied regions of the Confederacy. Some of it was purchased with gold that invariably found its way to blockade-running transfer ports in the Bahamas, or even to Northern towns like Cincinnati, where it was used to buy weapons for the Confederate army. During the Civil War, twice as much cotton was sold across enemy lines as was exported through the maritime blockade. In normal times New England's textile makers were tied with France as the second largest buyer of cotton feedstock but during the war they were the largest.[154]

Northerners also wanted America to regain the benefits of Southern exports which partially hid the size of America's trade deficits. During the four Civil War years when the Federal Union had limited access to Southern cotton the country compiled a cumulative $360 million deficit on merchandise trade, which approximated 25% of the value of her cumulative exports. That was bad enough but consider how Southern cotton exports minimized the deficit after the war. From 1860 to 1876, America had a merchandise trade deficit every year except 1874. Although the cumulative deficit of $750 million was sizeable, $2.8 billion in cotton exports minimized it. Without cotton exports the merchandise deficit would have been $3.6 billion, which was about

---

[153] David L. Cohn *The Life and Times of King Cotton*, 148-49, 155-56; Hodding Carter *The Angry Scar*, (New York: Doubleday, 1959), 321; Samuel Elliot Morison and Henry Steele Commager *The Growth of the American Republic: Volume Two*, Fourth Edition, 173; Matthew Josephson *The Robber Barons*, 93

[154] Stanley Lebergott, "Why the South Lost: Commercial Purpose in the Confederacy, 1861–1865," *Journal of American History*, v. 70, n. 1 (June 1983): 72–73; Robert F. Futrell, "Federal Trade with the Confederate States: 1861–1865" (PhD diss., Vanderbilt University, 1950), 83–84.

five times larger. During the sixteen-year period—including the Civil War when little cotton was available—cotton accounted for 60% of all U.S. exports notwithstanding that the South was still recovering from the devastation of the Civil War.[155]

The Northern aim to transform the South into an exploited internal colony was both an immediate and long-term success. In 1860 the region's per capita income was 72% of the national average. After the Civil War it dropped to 51% where it stayed until 1900, thirty-five years later. It did not recover to its 72% below average ranking until 1950, which was eighty-five years after the war ended. Few historians today have a genuine comprehension of the length and multiracial characteristics of postbellum Southern poverty. Although Southern poverty and cotton culture is commonly associated with blacks, as late as 1940 whites comprised two-thirds of the region's farmers who either rented their lands or were sharecroppers. According to a 1938 presidential economic report, about half of Southern white farmers were sharecroppers "living under economic conditions almost identical to those of Negro sharecroppers."

Shortly after the Great Depression began, the president of General Motors (Alfred P. Sloan) voluntarily slashed his annual salary from $500,000 to $340,000. His $160,000 cut was more than all the income taxes paid by Mississippi's two million residents that year. Widespread Southern poverty led to lower life expectancies, principally because of poor diets and unaffordable medical care. Sixty-five years after the end of the Civil War, South Carolina was the only state with as much as half of its population

---

[155] "Growth of the Cotton Industry," Available: https://tinyurl.com/y8u23c8h [Accessed: July 12, 2020]; U.S. Department of Commerce, Historical Statistics of the United Sates: Colonial Times to 1957: 537-38, Available: https://tinyurl.com/yc8mvmld Accessed: [July 11, 2020]

under the age of twenty in 1930. The statistic reflected low life expectancies due poor public health.[156]

From 1858 Republicans knew that the vast territories west of the Missouri River would eventually become free states even if America continued as a united country without a Civil War. After the shooting started the Party realized that if they won the war those same territories would spawn multiple Republican-controlled states. When Lee surrendered at Appomattox the Federal Union had twenty-five states compared to only eleven that would eventually rejoin from the former Confederacy. Republicans realized that they could get a veto-proof congressional majority by only temporarily establishing puppet regimes in the former Confederate states. They accomplished that by denying the vote to many ex-Confederates and simultaneously extending it to the recently freed slaves. President Grant was first elected in 1868 by virtue of the arrangement. Despite being a military hero, he only received a minority of the white popular vote when first elected President in 1868.

The Carpetbag regimes kept the Republicans in charge in Washington until they no longer needed the black vote. Consequently, after 1876 the GOP virtually abandoned the ex-slaves. Republican-controlled Nebraska and Colorado had already joined the Union in 1867 and 1876, respectively. The next seven states to join after 1876—North Dakota, South Dakota, Montana, Washington, Idaho, Wyoming, and Utah—were overwhelmingly white and generally Republican. Each of the seven, for example, sent two more Republicans to the United States Senate upon gaining statehood. Oklahoma would be the first Democrat state to gain statehood after the Civil War, which was over forty years after the war had ended. Thus, the typical 1876 Republican politician

---

[156] David Cohn *The Life and Times of King Cotton*, 244-245, 247-8; Franklin Roosevelt, *National Emergency Council: Report on the Economic Conditions of the South*, 46 (July 22, 1938) Available: https://tinyurl.com/ybakbzdt [Accessed: July 12, 2020]

realized that black votes would steadily decline in value in terms of retaining the Party's national control.

Republicans made one last gasp to allegedly support black Southerners in 1890. Realizing that Republican President Benjamin Harrison's 1892 re-election would be hard to win, Massachusetts Senator Henry Cabot Lodge sponsored a Force Bill that would enable a small number of petitioners to demand Federal supervision of elections in their district. The bill was targeted at the South in hopes of getting some of the states into the Republican column in 1892 by causing a bigger black voter turnout. Nevertheless, Republicans abandoned the bill in exchange for Southern support on the McKinley Tariff, which increased tariff protection for domestic manufactures to the highest level of the postbellum era to that date. White Southerners objected to the Force Bill because the election supervisors and marshals would be Republican, a Party they did not trust to conduct fair elections.[157]

[157] Lodge's support for black voters could more accurately be described as manipulation because the chief objective was to get Benjamin Harrison re-elected; Louis Hacker and Benjamin Kendrick *The United States Since 1865*, 74

CHAPTER 13: QUARANTINE

THE ONLY WAY that new slave states could be added after popular sovereignty failed to make Kansas a slave state in 1858 would be if America acquired territories in the Caribbean, Central America or Hawaii. Even if such territories were annexed, they would not likely have become slave states. That's because the free states had been steadily increasing their control of the Federal government during the 1850s. Faster population growth in the North indicated that the trend was likely to continue indefinitely. Slave state advocates would have a hard time getting a mere majority vote, and even less of a chance of getting a two-thirds Senate majority as required for an international treaty.

Everyone, including Southerners, knew that quarantining slavery in the South would eventually end it in all the states. Four years before the war started a visiting British journalist toured the South. Among others, he interviewed a former Mississippi governor who said, "To restrict slavery within certain limits looked a more harmless proposition than to abolishing it outright, but in reality, it was just as fatal. Room for the expansion of the 'institution' was, he said, an absolute necessity for the South. If the slaves became massed together, insubordination would be the result. . . Even now, he declared, many men could not lie down quietly at night. . . What would it be if the whites found themselves in a miserable minority?" He was speaking at a time when blacks significantly outnumbered whites in the Mississippi Delta. One county, for example, had six thousand slaves and only two-hundred-fifty whites. He feared a slave rebellion, especially one incited or financed by Northerners who would escape any consequences as they had with John Brown's

1859 failed insurrection. Under such circumstances, Southerners conceded much in the interest of national unity by accepting popular sovereignty as a governing principle for future state admissions. In return, Republicans unnecessarily offered only their dictatorial ban on slaves in the territories.[158]

Unfortunately, Republicans did not merely want to end slavery, they wanted to destroy the South. They hated the Southerner more than they loved America. Massachusetts Republican Edward Atkinson spoke for many in his Party when he characterized Southerners as either arrogant planters or "poor white trash." Historian James Oakes describes how the Republican containment plan with a cordon of free states surrounding the slave states would destroy the South by either a slave rebellion or class revolution.

> The borders of free soil would press ever closer to the edges of the cotton states—and the process of slavery's internal dissolution that had already taken place in the Border States would commence in the Deep South. The slaves, restless and increasingly anxious for their freedom, now pent up and concentrated in the cotton belt, would become rebellious and even revolutionary. As cotton lands were exhausted and outlets for expansion were closed off the already sickly slave economy would begin to collapse. The value of slave property would dwindle to nothing. The vise-like grip of the slaveholding minority within the southern states would give way as the slaveless white majorities asserted themselves ... A homegrown antislavery party would finally emerge in the heart of the slave country [to abolish slavery].[159]

Republicans were willing to risk war in order to destroy the South, but they were not willing to share the cost of emancipating

---

[158] Allan Nevins, *The Emergence of Lincoln: 1859-1861*, 159-60

[159] James Oakes, *The Scorpion's Sting*, (New York: W. W. Norton, 2014), 34-35; J. G. Randall & David Donald, *The Civil War and Reconstruction*, 66

slaves. Prior to the Civil War, the Northern states that freed the most slaves—New York, Pennsylvania and New Jersey—did so gradually and with loopholes. New York's 1798 law stipulated that every female slave child born after July 3, 1799 would be freed in 1824 whereas male slave children would be freed in 1827. Until then they remained the slaveowner's property. New Jersey's 1804 law was similar. Many New York and New Jersey slaveholders circumvented the law by selling their slaves in slave states such as Maryland and Virginia where the salves, and their offspring, would remain slaves. One study estimates that two-thirds of New York's 36,000 slaves were sold "to slave states farther South." In short, the Northerner states evaded the costs of emancipation by selling their slaves down the river to Southerners.

Moreover, every nineteenth century slaveholding society in the Western Hemisphere ended the practice gradually and peaceably, instead of abruptly. In the 1830s, Great Britain freed the slaves in her Western colonies, including those in the Caribbean. She compensated the slaveholders and thereafter required the slaves to serve years of apprenticeship. After America freed her slaves with the Thirteenth Amendment in 1865, Cuba and Brazil were the only two slaveholding countries in the Hemisphere. Both ended the practice slowly and peaceably more than twenty years after Appomattox. In fact, the only Western Hemisphere country that used a war to end slavery was the United States.

In 1973 Claudia Golden analyzed the possibilities of compensated emancipation for America in her "Economics of Emancipation" article in the *Journal of Economic History*. She concluded that all of the four million slaves in 1860 could have been immediately set free by compensating slaveholders $2.7 billion. Although the amount was equivalent to 65% of the 1860 GDP, it was only 27% of her estimated $10 billion cost for the Civil War. It was also equal to the $2.7 billion in Federal debt accumulated during the war through the sale of war bonds. Thus, it could have been paid-off just as readily as the actual war debt had been paid off in the postbellum years.

More significantly, however, Ms. Golden estimates that the cost of *gradual* emancipation would have been much lower. If a program beginning in 1860 emancipated the slaves thirty years later in 1890 an estimated 5.3 million slaves would be freed in the latter year. Given that the slaves would have had thirty years to earn their freedom, the 1860 capital compensation to slaveholders would have been only $340 million. To that might be added the loss of breeding-rights for female slaves amounting to $210 million. Thus, a thirty-year transition beginning in 1860 would have cost $550 million, which was only 20% as costly as immediate emancipation.[160]

Although most Republicans were loath to pay compensation, President Lincoln generally supported it. In April 1862, a year after the war started, he persuaded Congress to free the slaves in the District of Columbia by compensating slaveholders $300 for each slave. Even as late as February 1865 at the Hampton Roads Peace Conference three months before Appomattox, he told the Confederate representatives that he might offer $400 million in slaveholder compensation if the South would lay down her arms. When Secretary of State Seward, who was also attending, objected, Lincoln replied, "If it was wrong in the South to hold slaves, it was wrong in the North to carry on the salve trade and sell them to the South." He added that it would also be wrong to hold on to the wealth the North had procured by selling slaves to the South if the North took the slaves back again without compensation. Lincoln was describing a situation analogous to a merchant selling goods to a customer, keeping the cash, and later requiring the customer to forfeit the goods without even a partial refund.

---

[160] Claudia Goldin, "The Economics of Emancipation," *Journal Economic History* v. 30, n. 1 (March 1973), 68, 70-72, 74, 76-77, 80

After the conference, Lincoln drafted a bill to pay slaveholders $400 million in bonds. Half would be remitted on April 1, 1865 if all resistance to Federal authority had ceased. The other half would be paid on 1 July providing that the Thirteenth Amendment was ratified. When cabinet members challenged his so-called generosity, the President replied, "We are now paying $3 million a day [to fight the war]" thereby implying that the bonds would cost less than another five months of wartime government spending. Since the cabinet's sentiment prevailed, the draft was never sent to Congress.[161]

The year before Lincoln issued the 1862 Emancipation Proclamation, Czar Alexander II (1855-1881) emancipated the Russian serfs. Even though there were six times as many Russian serfs as American slaves, the serfs were freed without any war. To be sure, serfs were not chattel slaves, but they were tied to the land. Should the landlord deny a serf's request to move, the serf's situation was only slightly better than that of the American slave. Alexander accomplished serf freedom by including nobles in the planning. Thousands of officials participated in the preparation over five years. Finally, in 1861 after two hundred years of serfdom, ex-serfs were allowed to vote, marry whom they please, sue in court, trade freely and purchase property. As compensation, a central bank paid the nobility for the land allocated to the serfs who repaid the bank mortgage over time.[162]

In fairness to the Republicans, however, slaveholders were reluctant to end slavery, even if compensated. No doubt a big part of the reason was anti-black racial prejudice. In 1860 the eleven states that would form the Confederacy had nine million people,

---

[161] David Donald, *Lincoln*, 560; James B. Conroy, "The Hampton Roads Peace Conference. *Virginia Tech: Essential Civil War Curriculum*. Available: https://tinyurl.com/y3q25vhs [Accessed: July 21, 2020]

[162] Michael Lynch, "The Emancipation of the Russian Serfs: 1861," *History Review* (December 2003) Available: https://tinyurl.com/y6gtemru, [Accessed: July 21, 2020]

including 38% who were slaves. The black ratio in the first seven cotton states that organized the Confederacy was an even higher 46%. Few of the region's whites were prepared for the social equality that emancipation might bring. In fairness to Southerners, however, Northerners were no more prepared for social equality with blacks. Since only about one percent of the population in the states north of the Ohio River and the Mason Dixon Line were blacks, Northerners were mainly intent on keeping blacks in the South.

As noted in chapter four, when Indiana and Ohio were admitted as states their blacks were not allowed to own property. When French tourist Alexis de Tocqueville visited America in 1830, he observed that race prejudice was most obvious in the states that never had slavery whereas the races were more compatible in the South. When President Lincoln sent General Lorenzo Thomas into the lower Mississippi Valley during the Civil War to recruit black soldiers and develop a system to industriously employ the remaining former slaves he wrote, "It will not do to send [black refugees] . . . into the free states for the prejudices of the people of those states are against such a measure and have enacted laws against the reception of free negroes." After the Civil War, Massachusetts Congressman George Boutwell admitted that one reason he favored civil and voting rights for Southern ex-salves was to keep them out of the North. He even recommended that Florida and South Carolina be reserved exclusively for ex-salves. Before and during the war Lincoln repeatedly said that he did not think blacks could ever attain social equality with whites anywhere in America. During a wartime meeting with black leaders President Lincoln urged that blacks consider compensated emigration.[163]

---

[163] Gene Dattel, *Cotton and Race in the Making of America*, (Lanham, Md.: Ivan R. Dee, 2009), 211, 235; David Donald, *Lincoln*, 267

By the time Lincoln moved into the White House on March 4, 1861 the Republican Party was too full of hatred for the Southerner to desire peace. Perhaps because of his Kentucky family connections, Lincoln sometimes showed a capacity to break from the Party dogma. In his 1862 annual message he asked Congress to consider a constitutional amendment that would guarantee compensated emancipation to any state, including those in the Confederacy, if they would agree to abolish slavery by 1900. The abolitionists burst into wild fury. In the end, Lincoln had advanced only the abolitionists' good side. He died leaving their hatred of Southerners unchecked. With deliberate selfishness the Republican Reconstruction plan threw gasoline on the smoldering embers of the defeated South, igniting racial division when they should have concentrated on building racial cooperation.

Historian Thomas Fleming concluded that the Northerner's hatred of the South ultimately caused the Civil War. "For forty years, New England had sulked and defied the federal government in two wars, mocked President Jefferson's embargo, and conferred in Hartford on terms of disunion. At last [in 1861] they could combine patriotism with their hatred of the South" to destroy the people they hated. That hatred continues presently. It is promoted by the media, academia, Hollywood and weather-vane politicians. The destruction of Confederate statues across the South in year 2020 is not an erasure of history. It is a rewriting of it, to proclaim that the Southerner can have no virtue that matters, except a hatred of his ancestors. Less than a month before Appomattox, the Confederate Congress realized that surrender would result in "having the history of our struggle written by New England historians."[164]

[164] Thomas Fleming, *A Disease of the Public Mind*, 268, 297; Christopher Hollis, *The American Heresy*, (New York: Minton Balch & Company, 1930), 146

EPILOGUE

AT THIS WRITING, Western Civilization is under attack. During the last thirty-five years students have been taught to focus on the mistakes of Western culture instead of its accomplishments. As the most powerful nation in the West, America has been especially targeted for her faults. Many professors holding such viewpoints, who were not censored when they were themselves a minority, now strictly censor those who disagree with them. They banish speakers with contrary viewpoints from their campuses. The result is a culture dominated by an elite class that has two signature characteristics.

First, it would rather America fail than have leaders inconsistent with the tenets of Identity Politics that values people for their immutable characteristics, such as skin color and gender, instead of the content of their character. The only legally sanctioned racism lingering in America today is affirmative action. It mostly penalizes Asian and Jewish minorities, not blacks. It similarly disadvantages males instead of females notwithstanding that women are a majority, not a minority. The second characteristic of the governing elite is their eagerness to rewrite history to conform to their agenda until, as George Orwell put it, "Nothing exists except an endless present in which the [elite] Party is always right." Under such circumstances there will be no history beyond that which is vouchsafed to us in authorized books and on the plaques of approved statues which can be rewritten on a caprice by the ruling class.

Only the elites gain from a society based upon victimology. Those deemed to be victims will always seek more aid, which generally

161

takes the form of self-perpetuating government institutions managed by the elites and motivated to benefit themselves more than those they are supposed to help. It was so in the Soviet Union and it will be the same in America should Identity Politics be our destiny. Unfortunately, MLK's claim that "The arc of the moral universe is long but bends toward justice" is a mirage. If it were true there would have been no twentieth century genocide in Armenia, Germany, China, the Soviet Union and elsewhere. Mankind has always been flawed and sometimes the worst of us still gain power. Even the well-intentioned often become tyrannical after gaining power. Robespierre, for example, defended the Reign of Terror that followed the French Revolution as the tool of the virtuous—up to the moment that he was himself guillotined.

Today's predicament is at least partly the fault of twentieth century Southerners who failed to guard Confederate Heritage. As Shelby Foote explained in a 1987 interview when asked about the violence in the South during school integration in the 1950s and 60s: "I blame the 'decent people' for most of that. They did not want integration either but instead of accomplishing it in an orderly way—they stepped back and said, 'Let the riffraff take care of it.' In place after place they did that and whenever they did there was big trouble. . . [The decent people] were wrong. They were as wrong as could be and they know that now."

They similarly let racial bigots appropriate the Confederate Battle Flag as a banner of segregation. Presently, Southern white supremacists are a vanishingly small number. Nonetheless, together with their children and grandchildren the 'decent people' must endure the mob destruction of ancestral memorials while others stand by silently as a new and more toxic riffraff has taken to the streets. The thought police of year 2020 dictate that none of the Southerners who defended their homes 160 years ago could possess any virtue to negate the accusation that they fought to perpetuate slavery even though 70% of Confederate families did not own slaves.[165]

According to Princeton Law Professor Robert George, nearly all his students declare that they would have been abolitionists had they lived in the South in the late 1850s. But he shows that only the tiniest fraction of them, or any of us, would have spoken out against slavery, or lifted a finger to free the slaves. Most of them—and us— would have gone along. Many would have supported the slave system and happily benefitted from it. Here's how Professor George makes his point.

He tells the students that he will credit their abolitionist claims if they can show that in leading their present lives they have stood up for the rights of *unpopular* victims of injustice and where they have done so knowing:

1. They would be loathed and ridiculed by powerful individuals and institutions in our society and;
2. They would be abandoned by many of their friends and;
3. They would be shouted down with vile names and;
4. They would be denied valuable professional opportunities as a result of their moral witnessing and;
5. They might even lose their jobs after such witnessing.

In short, he challenged the students to show where they have— at risk to themselves and their futures—stood up for a cause that is unpopular within the elite sectors of today's society. It is a revealing challenge to students but would be even more illuminating if applied to academic historians. It evokes the ancient wisdom, "Courage is the rarest of virtues."

THE END

---

[165] Shelby Foote, William C Carter, Ed. *Conversations with Shelby Foote,* (Jackson: University of Mississippi Press, 1989), 263

BIBLIOGRAPHY

MEMOIRS, DIARIES, PERSONAL PAPERS

Barker, Jacob *The Life of Jacob Barker.* Washington City: Privately Published, 1855.

Beecher, Henry Ward. *Patriotic Addresses.* New York: Fords, Howard & Hulbert, 1891.

Madison, James. *The Writings of James Madison: 1790-1802.* Boston: G. P. Putnam, 1906.

"Pickering, Timothy to Cabot, George" (January 29, 1804). *The Founders Constitution: Chapter 7, Document 24.* University of Chicago Press. https://tinyurl.com/y8wdewn3

Seward, William H. *The Works of William H. Seward: Vol. 1.* New York: Redfield, 1853.

Stowe, Harriet Beecher. *Life of Harriet Beecher Stowe,* ed. Charles Stowe. London: S. Low, Martson, Searle & Rivington, 1889.

HISTORICAL DOCUMENTS

Buchanan, James "Fourth Annual Message to Congress." (December 3, 1860) https://tinyurl.com/ycjbypq2

Constitution of the United States. https://tinyurl.com/qevw4br

Democratic Platform, 1860 (Breckinridge faction). https://tinyurl.com/y8mcxcax

Democratic Platform, 1860 (Douglas faction). https://tinyurl.com/r7c3a5m

Lincoln, Abraham. "First Inaugural Address." (March 4, 1861) https://tinyurl.com/y9ac6tp5

_____. *Peoria Speech*, (October 16, 1854) https://tinyurl.com/yd2944bs

_____. *House Divided Speech*. (June 16, 1858) https://tinyurl.com/aq95z4v

National Emergency Council. *Report on Economic Conditions of the South*. July 25, 1938. https://tinyurl.com/ybakbzdt

Seward, William H. *Irrepressible Conflict Speech*. (October 25, 1858) https://tinyurl.com/6mn64o5

U. S. Bureau of Census. *1860 Census: Introduction.* https://tinyurl.com/kwvkpbk

U. S. Department of Commerce. "Historical Statistics of the United Sates: Colonial Times to 1957." Washington: U. S. Government Printing Office, 1960. https://tinyurl.com/yc8mvmld

U. S. Department of Commerce. "Historical Statistics of the United States: 1789-1945." Washington: U. S. Government Printing Office, 1949.

U. S. Department of Commerce. "Historical Statistics of the United States: Colonial Times to 1970: Part 2." Washington: U. S. Government Printing Office, 1975.

"U. S. Federal Government Revenues 1790-Present: 1975." *CRS Report of Congress*. https://tinyurl.com/ybvbxoor

Yale Law School. "Confederate Constitution." https://tinyurl.com/upv38lx

BOOKS AND COMPILATIONS

Adams, Charles. *When in the Course of Human Events*. Lanham, Md.: Rowman & Littlefield, 2000.

_____. *For Good and Evil*. Lanham, Md.: Rowman & Littlefield, 1993.

Agar, Herbert. *The Price of Union*. Boston: Houghton Mifflin, 1950.

Albion, Robert. *The Rise of New York Port: 1815-1860*. New York: Chas. Scribner & Sons, 1939.

Atkinson, Edward. *Cheap Cotton by Free Labor.* Boston: A. Williams & Company, 1861.

Bauer, K. Jack. *A Maritime History of the United* States. Columbia: University of South Carolina Press, 1988.

Benson, William. *A Political History of the Tariff.* Bloomington, In.: Xlibris, 2010.

Brands, H. W. *Heirs of the Founders.* New York: Doubleday, 2018.

_____. *Andrew Jackson: His Life and Times.* New York: Doubleday, 2005.

Carter, Hodding. *The Angry Scar.* New York, Doubleday, 1959.

Catton, Bruce. *Never Call Retreat.* London: Phoenix Press, 2001.

_____. *The Coming Fury.* London: Phoenix Press, 2001.

Cohn, David. *The Life and Times of King Cotton.* New York: Oxford University Press, 1956.

Cooper, William J., and Thomas Terrill. *A History of the South.* Vol. 2. 4th ed. Lanham, Md: Rowman & Littlefield, 2009.

Coulter, Merton. *The Confederate States of America.* Baton Rouge: LSU Press, 1959.

Dattel, Gene. *Cotton and Race in the Making of America.* Lanham, Md.: Ivan R. Dee, 2009.

Davis, William C. *Jefferson Davis: The Man and His Hour.* New York: HarperCollins, 1991.

Donald, David. *Lincoln.* London: Jonathan Cape, 1995.

Eisenschiml, Otto. *Why the Civil War?* Indianapolis, In.: Bobbs-Merrill, 1958.

Fleming, Thomas. *A Disease in the Public Mind.* Boston: DaCapo Press, 2013.

Foote, Shelby *The Civil War: A Narrative, Volume 1.* New York: Random House, 1957.

_____. Carter, William C., Ed. *Conversations with Shelby Foote*. Jackson: University of Mississippi Press, 1989.

Foreman, Amanda. *A World on Fire*. New York: Random House, 2010.

Fowler, William. *The Sectional Controversy*. New York: Charles Scribner, 1864.

Francis, Simkins and Roland, Charles. *A History of the South*. New York: Alfred A. Knopf, 1972.

Gallagher, Gary. *The Union War*. Cambridge: Harvard University Press, 2011.

Guelzo, Allen. *Redeeming the Great Emancipator*. Cambridge: Harvard University Press, 2016.

Hacker, Louis and Kendrick, Benjamin. *The United States Since 1865*. Appleton-Century-Crofts, 1949.

Hearn, Chester G. *Gray Raiders of the Sea*. Camden, Me.: International Marine Publishing, 1992.

Hesseltine, William B. *A History of the South: 1607-1935*. New York: Prentice Hall, 1936.

_____. *Ulysses Grant Politician*. New York: Dodd & Mead, 1935.

Hicks, John. *Populist Revolt*. Minneapolis: University of Minnesota Press, 1931.

Hoffer, Eric. *The True Believer*. New York: Harper & Row, 1951.

Hollis, Christopher. *The American Heresy*. New York: Minton Balch & Company, 1930.

Hummel, Jeffrey. *Emancipating Slaves, Enslaving Free Men*. Peru, IL: Open Court, 1996.

Irwin, Douglas. *Clashing Over Commerce: A History of U. S. Trade Policy*. Chicago: University of Chicago Press, 2017.

Johnson, Ludwell. *Division and Reunion*. New York: John Wiley & Sons, 1978.

Jones, Howard. *Blue and Gray Diplomacy*. Chapel Hill: University of North Carolina Press, 2010.

Kettell, Thomas. *Southern Wealth and Northern Profits*. New York: George & John Wood, 1860.

Klein, Maury. *Days of Defiance*. New York: Vintage Books, 1999.

Leigh, Philip "Preempting the Civil War" *Lee's Lost Dispatch and Other Civil War Controversies*. Yardley, Pa.: Westholme Publishing, 2015.

Madison, James. *The Writings of James Madison: 1790-1802*. Boston: G. P. Putnam, 1906.

Marvel, William. *Mr. Lincoln Goes to War*. Boston: Houghton-Mifflin, 2006.

_____. *Lincoln's Mercenaries*. Baton Rouge: LSU Press, 2018.

Maverick, Augustus. *Henry J. Raymond and the New York Press*. Hartford, Ct.: A. S. Hale, 1870.

McPherson, James. *Battle Cry of Freedom*. New York: Oxford, 1988.

Miller, John C. *The Federalist Era*. New York: Harper & Row, 1963.

Morison, Samuel Elliot and Commager, Henry Steel. *The Growth of the American Republic: Volume 1*. New York: Oxford University Press, 1962.

_____ *The Growth of the American Republic: Volume 2*. New York: Oxford University Press, 1962.

Nevins, Allan. *Ordeal of the Union: Fruits of Manifest Destiny 1847-1852*. New York: Charles Scribner's & Sons, 1947.

_____. *The Emergence of Lincoln: 1859-1861*. New York: Charles Scribner, 1950.

_____. *The Emergence of Lincoln: 1857-1859*. New York: Charles Scribner, 1950.

North, Douglass C. *The United States Balance of Payments.* Princeton: Princeton University Press, 1960. http://www.nber.org/chapters/c2491

Oakes, James. *The Scorpion's Sting.* New York: W. W. Norton, 2014.

Owsley, Frank. *King Cotton Diplomacy.* Chicago: University of Chicago Press, 1931.

Potter, David M. *The Impending Crisis.* New York: Harper Colophon, 1976.

Quadagno, Jill. *The Transformation of Old Age Security.* Chicago: University of Chicago Press, 1988.

Randall, James, and Donald, David. *The Civil War and Reconstruction.* Boston: D. C. Heath, 1961.

Schwab, John. *The Confederate States of America: 1861-1865 – A Financial and Industrial History.* New York: Charles Scribner & Sons, 1901.

Stampp, Kenneth *America in 1857: A Nation on the Brink.* New York: Oxford University Press, 1992.

_____. *The Causes of the Civil War.* New York: Touchstone, 1991.

Stanwood, Edward. *American Tariff Controversies of the Nineteenth Century.* Boston: Houghton-Mifflin, 1903.

Studenski, Paul and Krooss, Herman. *Financial History of the United States* (Beard Books, 2001).

Tarbell, Ida. *The Tariff in Our Times.* New York: Macmillan, 1911.

Taussig, F. W. *A Tariff History of the United States.* New York: G. P. Putnam, 1905.

Tucker, Leslie R. *Major General Isaac Ridgeway Trimble.* Jefferson, N.C.: McFarland, 2005.

Walton, Hanes : Puckett, Sherman : Deskins, Donald. *The African American Electorate: A Statistical History, Volume 1.* Thousand Oaks, Ca.: SAGE Publishing, 2012.

Watkins, James L. *Production and the Price of Cotton for 100 Years*, Washington, U.S. Government Printing Office, 1895.

White, Ronald C. *American Ulysses*. New York: Random House, 2016.

Wilson, Edmund. *Patriotic Gore*. New York: W. W. Norton, 1962.

Wise, Stephen R. *Lifeline of the Confederacy*. Columbia: University of South Carolina Press, 1988.

ARTICLES

Baily, Ronald "The Other Side of Slavery," *Agricultural History* 68, n. 2, (Spring 1994).

Berlin, Ira. "Book Review: The Scorpion's Sting by James Oakes." *The Washington Post*. (May 30, 2014). https://tinyurl.com/y8dwgyz8

Egerton, Douglas. "Its Origin Is Not a Little Curious." *Journal of Free Men of the Early Republic* 5, n.4 (Winter 1985).

Goldin, Claudia. "The Economics of Emancipation," *Journal Economic History* 30, n. 1 (March 1973). (66-85)

Goldin, Claudia and Lewis, Frank. "Economic Costs of the Civil War," *Journal Economic History* 35, n. 2 (June 1975).

Hill, William. "Prospective Purpose of the Tariff Act of 1789." *Journal of Political Economy* 2, n. 1 (December 1893)

Johnson, Ludwell. *Securing the Blessings: Today the South, Tomorrow?* https://tinyurl.com/y9wrd6er

_____. "Fort Sumter and Confederate Diplomacy." *The Journal of Southern History* 26, n. 4, (November 1960).

Jolt, Byron W. "The Relation of the Protective Tariffs to the Trusts." *Publications of the American Economic Association,* 3rd series. 8, n. 1 (Feb. 1907).

Lebergott, Stanley. "Why the South Lost: Commercial Purpose in the Confederacy, 1861–1865." *Journal of American History* 70, n. 1 (June 1983)

Smith, Karen R. "Resurrection, Uncle Tom's Cabin and the Reader Crisis." *Comparative Literature Studies* 33, n. 44, (1996)

Sylla, Richard. "Federal Policy, Banking Market Structure, and Capital Mobilization in the United States, 1863–1913." *Journal of Economic History* 29, no. 4 (Dec. 1969): 657-686.

DISSERTATIONS

Bolt, William K. "The Tariff in the Age of Jackson." PhD diss., University of Tennessee, 2010

Futrell, Robert. "Federal Trade with the Confederate States: 1861–1865." PhD diss., Vanderbilt University, 1950.

MISCELLANEOUS AND WEBSITES

Bancroft, Hubert H., Ed. *The Great Republic by Master Historians: Volume III.* https://tinyurl.com/y9ermtwr

Bloomberg News. "Why the U.S. Embraced the Jones Act a Century Ago." (October 16, 2017). https://tinyurl.com/ybkmrbbq

Columbia University. "Slavery and Emancipation in New York." https://tinyurl.com/y8e7u7vv

_____. "Columbia University and Slavery." https://tinyurl.com/y7a6cp7t

Conroy, James B. "The Hampton Roads Peace Conference. *Virginia Tech: Essential Civil War Curriculum.* https://tinyurl.com/y3q25vhs

Corbett, Scott : Janssen, Volker : Lund, John M. : Pfannestiel, Todd : Vickery, Paul and Waskiewicz, Sylvie "The Economics of Cotton," *OER Services: U. S. History.* https://tinyurl.com/y35fjnwk

DeBow's Review: v.30, issues 1–4, (January–April 1861). https://tinyurl.com/y8pe3w3b

Emmer, Pieter. "The Big Disappointment: The Economic Consequences of the Abolition of Slavery in the Caribbean, 1833–1888." *Institute for Historical Research.* 2007. https://tinyurl.com/ycwoe5ds

"Growth of the Cotton Industry." https://tinyurl.com/y8u23c8h

Harper, Doug. "Slavery or Tariff?" *The American Civil War.* http://slavenorth.com/cw/economics.htm

Holcomb, Julie. "The Abolitionist Movement." *Virginia Tech: Essential Civil War Curriculum.* https://tinyurl.com/ybzwmnsq

"House Vote No. 151 in 1860 (36th Congress)." *Govtrack.us.* https://tinyurl.com/trbzejx

Leigh, Philip. "Differences between U.S. and Confederate Constitutions." *Civil War Chat Blog.* https://tinyurl.com/yd7dfk9j

_____. "Why No Confederate Supreme Court?" *Abbeville Institute.* https://tinyurl.com/y9bzdg7m

_____. "Northern Response to Southern Secession." *Civil War Chat Blog.* https://tinyurl.com/y7runqtz

Lynch, Michael. "The Emancipation of the Russian Serfs: 1861," *History Review* (December 2003) https://tinyurl.com/y6gtemru

Niles' Weekly Register. Baltimore, Niles Register, 1816. https://tinyurl.com/yajwq2of

Oyez.org. https://tinyurl.com/y5e38cx6

Transportation Institute. "Maritime History." https://tinyurl.com/ycr7ynyp

Vidal, Gore. *Lecture to the National Press Club.* (March 19, 1988). https://www.c-span.org/video/?1708-1/proposals-improve-us-government

Williams, Walter. "Historical Ignorance and Confederate Generals," *Town Hall* (July 22, 2020) Available: https://tinyurl.com/y3kfa7st

Williamson, Samuel H. and Cain, Louis. "Measuring Slavery in 2016 Dollars." MeasuringWorth.com. https://tinyurl.com/gmclspn

Wilmot, David. "A Congressman 'Pleads the Case of White Men'," *HERB: Resources for Teachers.* https://tinyurl.com/y5fknbas

WTO (The) and GAAT: A Principled History. https://tinyurl.com/y79

INDEX

175

ABOUT THE AUTHOR

PHIL LEIGH holds an MBA from Northwestern University and a B.S. in Electrical Engineering from Florida Institute of Technology. The *New York Times* published twenty-four of his articles on the Civil War during the Sesquicentennial. He's authored six earlier books on the Civil War and Reconstruction including: *The Confederacy at Flood Tide, Trading With the Enemy, Co. Aytch, Lee's Lost Dispatch* and *Southern Reconstruction.* Leigh's publications with Shotwell include his book about Hot Springs, Arkansas during the gangster era, *The Devil's Town*, and a narrative of Ulysses Grant's Reconstruction Presidence, *U.S. Grant's Failed Presidency.*

For more information on the author, please visit Mr. Leigh's blog on Civil War Chat and his Author Page at Amazon.

AVAILABLE FROM SHOTWELL PUBLISHING

IF YOU ENJOYED THIS BOOK, perhaps some of our other titles will pique your interest. The following titles are currently available:

Mark C. Atkins
> *Women in Combat: Feminism Goes to War*

Joyce Bennett
> *Maryland, My Maryland: The Cultural Cleansing of a Small Southern State*

Jerry Brewer
> *Dismantling the Republic*

Andrew P. Calhoun, Jr.
> *My Own Darling Wife: Letters From a Confederate Volunteer [John Francis Calhoun]*

John Chodes
> *Segregation: Federal Policy or Racism?*
> *Washington's KKK: The Union League During Southern Reconstruction*

Paul C. Graham
> *Confederaphobia: An American Epidemic*
> *When the Yankees Come: Former South Carolina Slaves Remember Sherman's Invasion*

Joseph Jay
> *Sacred Conviction: The South's Stand for Biblical Authority*

Suzanne Parfitt Johnson
> *Maxcy Gregg's Sporting Journal 1842 - 1858*

James R. Kennedy
> *Dixie Rising: Rules for Rebels*
> *When Rebel Was Cool*

James R. Kennedy & Walter D. Kennedy

Punished with Poverty: The Suffering South

Yankee Empire: Aggressive Abroad and Despotic At Home

Philip Leigh

The Devil's Town: Hot Spring During the Gangster Era

U.S. Grant's Failed Presidency

John Marquardt

Around the World in Eighty Years: Confessions of a Connecticut Confederate

Michael Martin

Southern Grit: Sensing the Siege at Petersburg

Samuel W. Mitcham

The Greatest Lynching in American History: New York, 1863

Lewis Liberman

Snowflake Buddies: ABCs for Leftism for Kids!

Charles T. Pace

Lincoln As He Really Was

Southern Independence. Why War?

James Rutledge Roesch

From Founding Fathers to Fire Eaters: The Constitutional Doctrine of States' Rights in the Old South

Kirkpatrick Sale

Emancipation Hell: The Tragedy Wrought By Lincoln's Emancipation Proclamation

Karen Stokes

A Legion of Devils: Sherman in South Carolina

Carolina Love Letters

Leslie R. Tucker

Old Time There Should Not Be Forgotten: Cultural Genocide in Dixie

John Vinson

Southerner, Take Your Stand!

Howard Ray White

Understanding Creation and Evolution

How Southern Families Made America

Joe A. Wolverton, II

What Degree of Madness?" Madison's Method for Making American STATES Again

Walter Kirk Wood

Beyond Slavery: The Northern Romantic Nationalist Origins of America's Civil War

Clyde N. Wilson

Annals of the Stupid Party: Republicans Before Trump (The Wilson Files 3)

Lies My Teacher Told Me: The True History of the War for Southern Independence & Other Essays (Free eBook version available at www.freeliewsbook.com)

Nullification: Reclaiming Consent of the Governed (The Wilson Files 2)

Reconstruction and the New South: 50 Essential Books (Southern Reader's Guide III)

The Old South: 50 Essential Books (Southern Reader's Guide I)

The War Between the States: 60 Essential Books (Southern Reader's Guide II)

The Yankee Problem: An American Dilemma (The Wilson Files 1)

GREEN ALTAR BOOKS *(Literary Imprint)*

Catharine Savage Brosman

An Aesthetic Education and Other Stories

Chained Tree, Chained Owls: Poems

Randall Ivey

A New England Romance & Other SOUTHERN Stories

James Everett Kibler

Tiller (Clay Bank County, IV)

Karen Stokes

Belles: A Carolina Romance

Honor in the Dust

The Immortals

The Soldier's Ghost: A Tale of Charleston

Carolina Twilight

William A, Thomas, Jr.

Runaway Haley: An Imagined Family Saga

GOLD-BUG *(Mystery & Suspense Imprint)*

Michael Andrew Grissom
> *Billie Jo*

Brandi Perry
> *Splintered: A New Orleans Tale*

Martin L. Wilson
> *To Jekyll and Hide*

ShotwellPublishing.com

Made in the USA
Middletown, DE
06 August 2021